Bristol Radical Pamp͏ ͏ ͏ ͏ "͏

Yesterda
To-morrow

Bristol's Garden Suburbs

Steve Hunt

ISBN 978-1-911522-09-6

Bristol Radical History Group. 2nd Edition, 2015.
1st Edition, 2009.
www.brh.org.uk ~ brh@brh.org.uk

Acknowledgements

Thanks are due to John Roberts and other members of Save Sea Mills Garden Suburb for extensive advice when updating the section relating to Sea Mills. Andy Foyle provided advice for the section about St Annes. I am also grateful to Mike Houlden and Ian Haddrell for making available the drawing of a garden in the section on Lockleaze and to Tim Clench for sharing his unpublished essay about Fry's. Finally I extend my thanks to my comrade Di Parkin of the Bristol Radical History Group and Lynda Mansell for proof-reading and comments upon the text. As ever Rich Grove went more than the extra mile to pull it all together.

Picture Credits

Page 3: Shirehampton Bristol Garden Suburb, front cover from Prospectus. BRO RefNo 358 WWP F 19 c Bristol Record Office.

Page 6: Ebenezer Howard's 'Three Magnets' illustration from *Tomorrow: A Peaceful Path to Real Reform* (1898). Available from archive.org.

Page 12: Elizabeth Sturge (1850-1944). From *Elizabeth Sturge, Reminiscences of My Life: and some Account of the Children of William and Charlotte Sturge and of the Sturge Family of Bristol (1928)*. Reproduced with permission of Bristol Central Reference Library.

Page 13: Directors of the Bristol Garden Suburb, from Prospectus of the Bristol Garden Suburb, Shirehampton. BRO RefNo 358 WWP F 19 c Bristol Record Office.

Page 14: Proposed Group of Four Cottages from Prospectus of Bristol Garden Suburb, Shirehampton. BRO RefNo 358 WWP F 19 c Bristol Record Office.

Page 15: Shirehampton Bristol Garden Suburb, furniture advertisement from Prospectus. BRO RefNo 358 WWP F 19 c Bristol Record Office.

Page 15: Passage Leaze, Shirehampton in 2014. Photograph by Stephen E. Hunt.

Page 17: Layout of proposed garden suburb, map from Prospectus , Shirehampton. BRO RefNo 358 WWP F 19 c Bristol Record Office.

Page 20: Old Quarry Road, Penpole Housing Estate, Shirehampton nd[1950s]. BRO RefNo 40826/HSG/138/1 Bristol Record Office.

Page 22: Sea Mills Square with St Edyths Church. Photograph by Stephen E. Hunt.

Page 30: Maple Avenue, Hillfields. Photograph by Stephen E. Hunt.

Page 32: Filwood Broadway, Knowle West. Photograph by Stephen E. Hunt.

Page 34: Filwood Broadway Cinema, Knowle West. Photograph by Stephen E. Hunt.

Page 36: Trowbridge Road, Southmead. Photograph by Stephen E. Hunt.

Page 38: 'Pride of Southmead', Southmead Youth Centre. Photograph by Stephen E. Hunt.

Page 40: View of rear garden 4 Haydon Gardens, Lockleaze, 1961. Supplied and reproduced with kind permission from Michael Houlden who originally drew it for a school homework assignment. This first appeared in Ian Haddrell, *Lockleaze Schools* (2008), 125.

Page 43: Fry's souvenir tin. Photograph by Stephen E Hunt.

Page 45: Fry's chocolate factory Somerdale. From a pamphlet called *Fry's of Bristol* (and undated) in Frenchay Library, University of the West of England.

Page 47: *Fry's Works Magazine 1728-1928* [Bi-Centenary Number], ed. by W. T. Pearce (Bristol: Partridge & Love, [1928]).

Page 51: "New Housing Estate, Sea Mills". *Souvenir of the Trades Union Congress at the Victoria Rooms Bristol September 1931*. Ed. Charles Wittarding

The BRISTOL GARDEN SVBVRB *Shirehampton*

In a moment of serendipity while rummaging in the Bristol Records Office I found the prospectus for a garden suburb for Shirehampton. I was struck by the relevance that such a project still has for present concerns with sustainable and sociable communities more than a century later. The Bristol Garden Suburb Limited was set up to implement the ideas Ebenezer Howard popularised in *To-morrow: A Peaceful Path to Real Reform* first published in 1898, subsequently reissued under the better known title *Garden Cities of To-morrow* (1902). A second area, nearby Sea Mills, was a more much extensive development inspired by garden-city ideas about planning. Furthermore a huge belt of inter-war municipal housing estates around the periphery of Bristol were also planned and constructed according to garden-city principles, albeit of a diluted version, thereby substantially defining the character of many of the city's residential areas up to the present day.

Influenced by the likes of William Morris and Peter Kropotkin, garden-city idealists such as Ebenezer Howard and Raymond Unwin sought to use planning to achieve economic well being, a healthy environment, robust and aesthetically appealing architectural design and an enabling infrastructure of services, thereby democratising the good life for all. Howard, a shorthand reporter and a dabbler in many things, prefigured radical ideas of dweller control far more progressive than those proposed in the early Twenty-First Century, such as the new generation of so-called garden-cities advocated by David Cameron's Coalition government at the time of writing in 2014. Current proposals for locations such as Ebbsfleet, suggest that the original garden-city philosophy will be diluted and distorted into conventional commuter-belt estates developed by volume house builders.

The approach in this pamphlet broadly but cautiously favours the progressive nature of garden-city thinking. As we shall see, however, the impact of such ideas upon the garden suburbs of Bristol during the early Twentieth Century shows some of the practical deficiencies of the garden-city vision as well as its desirability. The contrasting experience of several estates indicates the necessity to take a holistic approach to urban

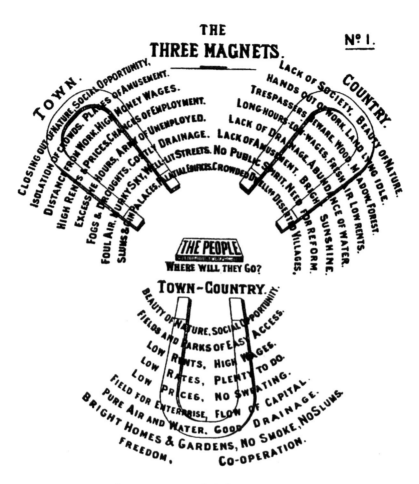

Ebenezer Howard's 'Three Magnets'.

design, so that residential zones are integrated with facilities, support services and public spaces. We also see that the attitudes of residents in the estates are not homogeneous. This raises fundamental questions about the nature of 'community', a slippery term which everyone across the political spectrum from greens and anarchists to conservatives professes to admire, but no one entirely trusts.

The appearance of the garden-suburb idea in Shirehampton before World War I, gives a fascinating insight into early twentieth-century planning and housing reform, offering practical and utilitarian solutions to immediate social ills while attempting to advance a progressive, even utopian impulse towards social change. Howard spoke of 'the task which is before us of reconstructing anew the entire external fabric of society'.[1] The garden-city movement continued to have a defining impact on Bristol's development after the First World War. Yet while the inspiration of Howard continued during the Interwar period, the garden-cities influence was much diluted in the municipal housing schemes that circled the city by 1939 and the 'garden factory' at Keynsham. Now discussion of garden cities has returned to national planning agendas, it is an appropriate moment to look at the significant if often overlooked impact that the movement had on the Bristol area during the early Twentieth Century. It's timely to revisit Howard's ideas in the light of several recent topics of green chatter – transition towns, sustainable planning and current debates about the viability of a renaissance in garden-city style development.

What are garden cities?

So what do I mean when I am talking about garden-city principles? Based on Howard's ideas, I would include the following features. These provide something of a benchmark against which to measure the quality of present-day garden-city proposals.

The core idea was to create deliberately planned, holistic communities or what Howard called Social Cities, combining residential areas with light industry. They are perhaps the opposite of a suburb as we now understand it in the term 'Suburbia' which has become byword for dull dormitory residential areas. Garden cities and suburbs were conceived as places where work and community were radically integrated.

Howard envisioned that these communities would have an optimum of around 32, 000 people, with surrounding agricultural production and green belt land. They would be human scale – ideally everything in the garden city would be in easy walking or cycling distance. This would reduce time and energy spent in commuting and erase the separation of home and work, making it possible to know neighbours and enable face-to-face communication which would in turn facilitate forms of self-government and direct democracy. These settlements would be coordinated

1 Ebenezer Howard, *Garden Cities of To-Morrow* [1902] (London: Faber, 1965), 150.

and federated. Howard's idea was that one garden city would be linked to other clusters of garden cities by trams, in a sort of advanced transit system. This wasn't therefore an attempt to embrace primitivism.

There would be a strong infrastructure of amenities such as schools, hospitals, community centres, libraries, museums, nurseries, allotments, sports facilities and recreational grounds (the inclusion of pubs and religious buildings was more debatable).

Howard aimed to bring together the positive aspects of town and country. He wished to avoid rural- and inner-city deprivation by making available the amenities and opportunities of town life as well as the benefits of accessible countryside with space for recreation and contact with the natural world. As depicted in his famous image of the three magnets, he believed that people are pulled by different needs for the cultural dynamism of the town and desire for space and recreation in the countryside, the town-county magnet, therefore, would have the greatest magnetic attraction because it attempted to reconcile competing needs.

There was a strong emphasis on excellent design, with attempts to combine the attractive aesthetics of the arts and crafts movement with the functional benefits of ergonomic considerations. The chief planners and architects of the garden cities movement – such as partners Barry Parker and Raymond Unwin, and also Thomas Adams (involved at Shirehampton and Sea Mills) – were linked to the Arts and Crafts Movement with libertarian socialist views in the tradition of William Morris and Ebenezer Howard.

The post-War Tudor Walters Report (1918), which was heavily influenced by the garden cities movement and the popular demand for 'Homes fit for Heroes', fed into the *Housing and Town Planning Act 1919* (the 'Addison Act') and the first Labour government's *Housing (Financial Provisions) Act 1924* (the 'Wheatley Act') which stipulated that there should be a density of 12 houses per acre. Robust design and quality of materials made them cheaper to maintain and so helped to keep rental costs down. As we shall see, sometimes the approach to construction was experimental such as the use of PRC Parkinson concrete at Sea Mills and Horfield.

The urge to standardise production to meet mass demand where necessary was combined with an insistence that developments should be varied in design and not homogenous. Neighbourliness could be encouraged by culs-de-sac, houses had ample gardens for self-sufficiency, and were separated by avenues and village greens and other features such as focal points were incorporated. In the Sea Mills estate to the west of Bristol, for example, there were conscious attempts to make the most of light and sun by south-facing alignments and exploit natural topography by making most of features such the Avon Gorge and Welsh hills.

It was seen as important to create a healthy human environment while protecting the natural environment. Garden cities would be surrounded by green belt land to prevent planning sprawl (for purists, garden suburbs represented something of a break with this objective). Healthy environments would include open spaces for play and recreation and no polluting industries, and measures to filter chimney stacks in keeping with demands of the late Victorian Smoke Abatement Society.

Community leasing was a key and distinguishing feature of garden cities. Economists such as Henry George advocated a progressive land tax – those with most land would pay most, thus facilitating greater social equality (the tax being paid to the state). Howard, in keeping with Peter Kropotkin and William Morris, took a more decentralised approach – in the garden cities residents would lease their homes and gardens from the community and the resulting income would be retained by the community so that wealth stayed local. Using a system of tenant co-ownership, expenditure and investment would then be decided by garden city trustees, democratically elected by the residents. Aiming to end property speculation for profit, Community leasing was considered as an alternative to state control or private ownership. In providing mixed housing to accommodate different incomes, Howard took a reformist rather than revolutionary approach that looked towards the gradual convergence of class difference. In this way, it was, perhaps naïvely hoped, that the common ownership of land and means of production would eventually entail the demise of a situation in which a separate capitalist class owns the means of production and exploits real wealth creators by accruing surplus value and would thus address economic alienation.

In keeping with this decentralised approach there was an emphasis on self-contained, autonomous decentralised communities with an ethos of self-government and cooperative principles.

Yesterday

It is fitting that garden suburbs were to have an impact on Bristol, being the site of Blaise Hamlet, an early attempt to achieve humanitarian ends through planning and architecture. After the first shock of the Industrial Revolution during the Romantic period, many of the issues that the garden-city movement raised were already in place: the impact of environmental conditions and aesthetic circumstances on individual and community well-being, paternalism versus worker autonomy, the constraints of power and ownership on workers' decision making.

The Bristolian banker John Scandrett Harford (1785-1866) financed the construction of Blaise Hamlet for older residents, the architectural design being undertaken by John Nash (1752-1835) and George Repton (1786-1858). The late eighteenth-century enthusiasm for the bucolic and picturesque inspired the deliberately asymmetrical thatched dwellings near Henbury where the project was completed in 1810. The designs were intended to be aesthetically pleasing, solidly constructed and in keeping with fashionable contemporary theories about the picturesque. Rounded, thatched dwellings of this kind conform perfectly to the nest-like curvature and cosiness that the French philosopher Gaston Bachelard suggested were archetypal forms meeting primal human needs for belonging, comfort and security in his classic study *The Poetics of Space* (1958). The rustic brickwork, timbers and trellises of Blaise Hamlet were crafted not only with aesthetic considerations but also with political and religious motivations. Historian Gillian Darley records that Harford was a Quaker whose humanitarian ideas made him an energetic anti-slavery campaigner and prison reformer, making it clear that he was inspired by his faith and a desire for social improvement in the creation of Blaise Hamlet.[2]

---

2 Gillian Darley, *Villages of Vision: A Study of Strange Utopias*, rev. and updated edn (Nottingham: Five Leaves, 2007), 68. I have drawn upon Darley's fascinating book for the factual details about Blaise Hamlet above.

Shirehampton

Elizabeth Sturge (1850-1944) and Eliza Walker Dunbar (1845-1925) instigated the Shirehampton garden suburb in 1907. This was planned as a modest, scaled-down version of its more ambitious cousin the garden city, exemplified in the developments at Letchworth and Welwyn Garden City. An earlier development instigated by George White to the north of the city at Filton Park, had also been described as a 'garden suburb'.[3] In practice however, while it featured a low density of occupation, White's project reflected only a limited aspiration to implement garden-city principles since it had a conventional set-up in terms of funding and ownership.[4] Howard's approach more directly inspired the Shirehampton scheme as it attempted to take practical measures to provide working people with affordable, high-quality homes in a healthy environment.

Elizabeth Sturge had first-hand experience of housing poverty as an assistant to Octavia Hill in Southwark during the 1880s. Octavia Hill was already a notable figure in housing reform since John Ruskin had given her inspiration and capital to ease London housing poverty.[5] Back in Bristol Elizabeth Sturge's long-term commitment to improving housing conditions continued through her membership of the Bristol Committee for the Better Housing of the Poor at the beginning of the Twentieth Century.[6] A member of a humanitarian Quaker family, Elizabeth was also a prominent campaigner for votes for women, alongside her sisters Helen and Caroline. Eliza Dunbar was one of the first women to enter the exclusive medical profession as surgeon and was a member of the Bristol Association of Working Women.[7] Their intervention in the public

3 George White was prominent as Chair of the Bristol Tramways Company and due to his wider role in Bristol's transport and industry. For his notorious anti-union record, see Mike Richardson, *Bristol and the Labour Unrest of 1910-14*, Bristol Radical Pamphleteer #27 (Bristol: Bristol Radical History Group, 2013), 10.

4 Keith J. Skilleter, 'Housing Reform, Garden Suburbs and Statutory Town Planning at Bristol, 1900-39', pp. 12-23 of *Planning History* 13.2 (1991), 14.

5 Elizabeth Sturge, *Reminiscences of My Life: and some account of the children of William and Charlotte Sturge and of the Sturge Family of Bristol* (Bristol: printed by J. A. Arrowsmith for private circulation, 1928), 45-46.

6 Moira Martin, 'Guardians of the Poor: A Philanthropic Female Elite in Bristol', *Regional Historian* 9 (Summer 2002), 11.

7 Biographical details gleaned from Lorna Brierley and Helen Reid, *Go Home and Do the Washing! Three Centuries of Pioneering Bristol Women* (Bristol: Broadcast Books, 2000).

Elizabeth Sturge (1850-1944)

arena of housing shows that middle-class women could be instrumental in local political reform despite being excluded from the franchise.

Following Ebenezer Howard's inspiration, a board of seven directors was set up, including Elizabeth Sturge and Eliza Dunbar, to raise £10, 000 to fund a development at Shirehampton. This was to be achieved through the sale of 10, 000 £1 shares for the purchase of 26½ acres of land, from Philip Napier Miles, the last squire of the King's Weston Estate.[8] The King's Weston Action Group record philanthropist Philip

8 'Shirehampton Garden Suburb prospectus', 2. Bristol Record Office, MS Bristol Plans Numbered/62. Ref: 07784/62.

The Directors and Officers of the Company are as follows :—

Directors :

FRANCIS NICHOLAS COWLIN, ESQ., of Messrs. William Cowlin & Son, Builders and Contractors Stratton Street, St. Paul's, Bristol.

MISS ELIZA LOUISA WALKER DUNBAR, M.D., 9, Oakfield Road, Clifton.

FREDERICK ALLEN STURGE GOODBODY, ESQ., of Messrs. J. P. Sturge & Sons, Land Agents and Surveyors, 33, Corn Street, Bristol.

HENRY HOSEGOOD, ESQ., of Messrs. Henry Hosegood & Son, Corn Merchants, 3, Queen Square, Bristol.

MONTAGUE MUIR MACKENZIE, ESQ., J.P., Penpole House, Shirehampton, near Bristol.

GEORGE HERBERT OATLEY, ESQ., F.R.I.B.A., 25, Orchard Street, Bristol.

MISS ELIZABETH STURGE, Heathlands, Leigh Woods, Clifton.

Solicitors : PAGE & THOMPSON, 2, Bristol Chambers, Nicholas Street, Bristol.

Surveyors : J. P. STURGE & SONS, 33, Corn Street, Bristol.

Secretary and Registered Office :

A. ERNEST ASHMEAD, Chartered Accountant, Exchange Chambers, Bristol.

Resident Architect : FRANK H. BROMHEAD, A.R.I.B.A.

Directors of the Bristol Garden Suburb.

Napier Miles's major impact on the Shirehampton area by selling land and making donations for significant community assets such as the Public Hall and Library and the King's Weston Estate Office, both designed by architect (and later Glastonbury mystic) Frederick Bligh Bond.[9] Philip Napier Miles's grand-father, Philip John Miles (1773-1845), a member of the Merchant Venturers, originally amassed much of the Miles family fortune. Steve Livings described Philip John Miles as 'Bristol's first recorded millionaire', a wealth derived through interests in shipping, sugar plantations and banking.[10] If the ethical provenance of wealth from such interests at this time is starting to sound doubtful, the King's Weston Action Group confirm that the Miles family wealth was in part derived from 'extensive plantations in Trinidad and Jamaica' – and hence was tainted by its source in both direct slave labour and the trans-Atlantic slave trade (and substantially enhanced by compensation when the trade was abolished).[11]

9 King's Weston Action Group website, 'Philip Napier Miles: Philanthropy and Music': http:// www.kwag.org.uk/history/philip-napier-miles/ [accessed 29 March 2014].

10 Steve Livings, 'The Miles Family and Leigh Court': http://www.abbotsleigh.org.uk/ALMiles. html [accessed 29 March 2014].

11 King's Weston Action Group website, 'The Victorian Era: The Miles Family': http://www. kwag.org.uk/history/the-victorian-era/ [accessed 29 March 2014]. See also UCL Department of History's Legacies of British Slave-ownership webpage for Philip John Miles: http://www.ucl. ac.uk/lbs/person/view/19118 [accessed 29 March 2014].

"Proposed Group of Four Cottages, Passage Leaze."

The financial administration was put on a firm footing by the creation of the Bristol Garden Suburb Limited, specifically founded for this purpose in 1909. The prospectus follows the meticulously costed structural model and principles set out in *Garden Cities of To-morrow*. Indeed Howard endorsed the project personally by attending an inaugural meeting organised by Alfred Lyttleton to promote the scheme at the Victoria Rooms, Clifton in 1908.[12] Henrietta Barnett, wife of Bristol-born housing reformer Samuel Augustus Barnett, also spoke in Bristol the following year.[13] She was the founder of the fine Hampstead Garden Suburb which dates from 1907. Based upon Howard's ideas and put into practice by planner and architect Raymond Unwin the scheme in Hampstead was the immediate inspiration for the development in Shirehampton.

While there would be some diversity in the size and design of the dwellings, the Shirehampton prospectus promised generously adequate open spaces and a 'capital garden' for each. In anticipation of present-day initiatives for 'mixed housing', the prospectus set out the intention to build 'houses for all classes' on the site. The drive towards economic

12 Skilleter, 'Housing Reform…', 14.
13 Sarah Whittingham, *Sir George Oatley: Architect of Bristol* (Bristol: Redcliffe Press, 2011), 284.

SIMPLE FURNITURE.

Shirehampton Bristol Garden Suburb,
furniture advertisement from Prospectus.

Passage Leaze in 2014.

self-sufficiency is an important part of Howard's programme, which intended that residents of the garden cities would live within walking distance of their workplace. For Howard, the garden cities were to have an optimum size of 32, 000 residents; above this size a second garden city would be initiated to maintain surroundings with a human scale. Howard hoped that clusters of such communities would soon emerge, linked by integrated public transport such as municipal railway systems to avoid the sense of social isolation often suffered by small-town and rural communities lacking public amenities in his own time, and to this day. It was also anticipated that the local Co-operative Societies, with their roots in Owenite socialism, would play a supportive and mutually benefit role. The creators of the Shirehampton suburb equally looked to sub-contract the construction work to local builders, Co-operative Societies or ideally to a complementary building company that might be founded for the purpose. The intention that the project should combine elements of limited profit making and philanthropy is enshrined in the founding statement: 'The rate of dividend on the Shares has been limited to 5 per cent. in the belief that many persons will be satisfied with a moderate return in connection with a social experiment of great importance'.[14]

It is easy to be unaware of this gradualist but thoroughgoing attempt at social transformation when strolling past the houses in Passage Leaze in Shirehampton today. However, the distinctive dormer windows and cottage-style appearance, owing much to the Victorian Arts and Crafts Movement – (one is called Morris Cottage, presumably after William Morris) – unmistakeably resemble the gabled dwellings that appear in the original prospectus. The project got off to a promising start in 1907 when Thomas Adams (1871-1940) drew up plans for nearly three hundred homes. Adams was to become a significant practitioner and authority on twentieth-century planning. His mapping of the terrain at Shirehampton was complemented by the young architect Frank Harold Bromhead's (1882-1972) attractively designed houses. Sarah Whittingham records that by this date Bromhead had already worked at Letchworth and Hampstead Garden Suburb with the prominent garden-city architects

14 'Shirehampton Garden Suburb prospectus', 2.

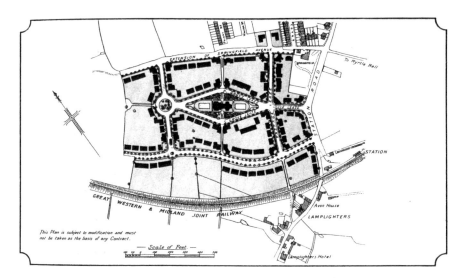

Layout of the proposed garden suburb in Shirehampton.

Barry Parker and Raymond Unwin.[15] Unfortunately the project had only made limited progress when the work was suspended due to the outbreak of hostilities in the First World War. Ewart Culpin recorded that just 44 out of a planned 280 houses had been completed when he was writing in 1913.[16] 'It was a shame that the whole of the Shire wasn't built like it, but I suppose the Kaiser had something to do with that!' a Passage Leaze resident with an obvious affection for his home and street told me. While the existing arrangements continued after the War, the house-building plan was not revived and the Bristol Garden Suburb Company was taken over by the Bristol Housing Company in 1923. More than 900 further houses were built in the larger estate constructed in the decade after 1920. Sadly, quality of design and planning was reduced in this larger municipal development and today 'the Shire', while retaining a strong community spirit, is an area of high deprivation with few of the amenities and opportunities enjoyed in more prosperous urban areas of Bristol or the compensations of more picturesque rural districts.[17]

15 Whittingham, *Sir George Oatley*, 285.
16 Ewart G. Culpin, *The Garden City Movement Up-to-Date* (London: Garden Cities and Town Planning Association, 1913), 48.
17 See Ian Bone, *Community Profile of Shirehampton* (Bristol: Shirehampton Public Hall Community Association, 2001). Viewed online at http://www.digitalbristol.org/members/shireweb/hall/profile.htm [Accessed 8 June 2007].

17

Quality of life and well-being were to be a central feature of the original development at Shirehampton. Applications to set up light industry were welcomed with the proviso that 'factories are fitted with up-to-date appliances for the prevention of smoke and fumes emanating therefrom'.[18] The avoidance of overcrowding and pollution had also been understood to be a powerful and benign form of social conditioning since the pioneering work of social observers such as Henry Mayhew and Charles Booth. Howard speaks of lives being 'stunted and maimed' by the darkness and confinement of overcrowding, taking the natural metaphor of pot-bound plants who can only flourish when transplanted.[19] The environmental model for human health was in common currency in progressive discourse during the 1890s. There proved to be a persuasive evidence base for this – Gillian Darley notes that one survey of Bournville children in the early Twentieth Century found them to be 'two to three inches taller there than in slum areas of Birmingham'.[20]

Robert Blatchford, an influential socialist writer, was forthright on the matter, describing the present condition of workers' 'very ugly and *mean*' houses:

The streets are too narrow. There are no gardens. There are no trees. Few working-class families have enough bedrooms, and the bathroom is a luxury not known in cottages.

In fine, your houses are ugly, unhealthy, inconvenient, dark, ill-built, ill-fitted, and dear.[21]

Madge Dresser's study of working-class housing in Bristol reveals that many central districts, characterised by the notorious courts and tenement lodging houses, fitted Blatchford's description. At the beginning of the Twentieth Century many areas were blighted by overcrowding, poverty and extremely unsanitary conditions.[22] By contrast Blatchford

18 'Shirehampton Garden Suburb prospectus', p. 2.
19 In an early manuscript entitled 'Commonsense Socialism' quoted in Robert Beevers, *The Garden City Utopia: A Critical Biography of Ebenezer Howard* (Basingstoke: Macmillan, 1988), 31.
20 Darley, *Villages of Vision*, 140.
21 Robert Blatchford, *Merrie England* (London: Clarion Office, 1894), 41.
22 Madge Dresser, 'People's Housing in Bristol (1870-1939)', pp. 129-160 in *Bristol's Other History*, ed. by Ian Bild (Bristol: Bristol Broadsides, 1983).

imagines a transformed public space if the potential for better planning could be realised:

> I would have the towns rebuilt with wide streets, with detached houses, with gardens and fountains and avenues of trees. [...] I would make the houses loftier and larger, and clear them of all useless furniture. I would institute public dining halls, public baths, public wash-houses on the best plans, and so set free the hands of those slaves – our English women.[23]

In common with other socialists with temperance leanings, Blatchford regretted 'drunkenness' as one of the scourges of the working class.[24] John Roberts notes that pubs are absent from nearby Sea Mills 'in keeping with the ethos of a garden suburb as a healthy and wholesome place to live'.[25] Indeed pubs were notable by their absence throughout Bristol's municipal housing estates during the 1920s, a cause for complaint on the part of many corporation residents, often to be circumvented by the entrepreneurial spirit of a fleet of vans that supplied tenants with alcohol, presumably on the black market.[26]

A feature that distinguished garden cities and suburbs from their antecedents in model housing schemes, created by philanthropic industrialists, such as Titus Salt's Saltaire, George Cadbury's Bournville and the Lever brothers' Port Sunlight, was the degree of community ownership by the residents. Gillian Darley tellingly quotes a union official who commented 'no man of an independent turn of mind could breathe for long in the atmosphere of Port Sunlight'.[27] Thomas Adams, involved in the Shirehampton development and Secretary of the national Garden City Association, noted the significance of this break from 'paternalism' to-

23 Blatchford, *Merrie England*, 43.
24 Blatchford, *Merrie England*, 16.
25 John Roberts, *The Definition and Characteristics of a Post-WWI Garden Suburb with Particular Reference to Sea Mills Garden Suburb, Bristol: A Study by Save Sea Mills Garden Suburb in association with Sea Mills and Coombe Dingle Community Project* (Bristol: Save Sea Mills Garden Suburb/Sea Mills and Coombe Dingle Community Project, 2007), 49.
26 Madge Dresser, 'Housing Policy in Bristol, 1919-30', pp. 155-216 in *Councillors and Tenants: Local Authority Housing in English Cities 1919-1939*, ed. by M. J. Daunton (Leicester: Leicester University Press, 1984), 208.
27 Darley, *Villages of Vision*, 142.

wards an administrative structure that optimised economic autonomy and self-administration.[28] He would have had in mind intrusions such as the overbearing surveillance of Titus Salt who had a watchtower constructed which acted as a kind of panopticon from which he could survey his employees with God-like omniscience, ever watchful for drinking or the illicit hanging of laundry on visible washing lines.

Avonmouth

Meanwhile at nearby Avonmouth plans for a major development of up to 1200 workers' houses were drawn up under the auspices of Avonmouth Garden Suburbs Ltd. during the War years. These had the enthusiastic support of the Dock, Wharf, Riverside and General Workers Union and the expertise of an equally enthusiastic Garden Cities and Town Planning Association (GCTPA). Working-class labour activists Frank Sheppard, Ernest Bevin and Ben Tillett supporting the scheme had been advocating the provision of communal kitchens and nurseries as rational time saving

Old Quarry Road, Penpole Housing Estate.

28 Thomas Adams in collaboration with F. Longstreth Thompson, E. Maxwell Fry and James W. R. Adams, *Recent Advances in Town Planning* (London: J. & A. Churchill, 1932), 37.

measures and to improve the situation of working-class women.[29] These were progressive demands fully in keeping with the ideas of Blatchford and Howard. This promising and enlightened scheme was to be created by a co-operative but, in what was to become a familiar pattern, floundered in meeting its goals due to limited capital.[30] Only 150 houses were built in a more conventional estate for the war-time Ministry of Munitions. Despite the input of Ewart Culpin, Secretary of the GCTPA, in drawing up an advanced master plan for a much grander development at Avonmouth that was to include 'social and educational centres, several large shopping centres, swimming-baths, gymnasia and allotments', the scheme was dropped in favour of the municipal Penpole housing estate, which owed only its low-density of development and spacious gardens to the garden-city movement.[31] Richard Coates cites the 1920's Penpole Estate as including houses around The Ridge, Grumwell Close and Old Quarry Road.[32]

Sea Mills: The 'magic estate'

If the garden suburb at Shirehampton was to be thwarted by the outbreak of the First World War, then a larger development at nearby Sea Mills was to owe its advent to the bid to build 'homes fit for heroes' in the form of 'village suburbs' in the aftermath of the War. Dave Backwith records that 'before the war had ended Bristol Council had approved plans and was buying land for 5, 000 houses to be built in garden suburbs at Fishponds (Hillfields), Horfield, Sea Mills, Shirehampton and Knowle'.[33] Additional developments took place at Bedminster Down, St Anne's, Southmead, Speedwell and St George.

The new development at Sea Mills delighted the poet John Betjeman. Reporting for the BBC in 1937, he described:

29 Dresser, 'Housing Policy in Bristol, 1919-30', 168.
30 Dresser, 'Housing Policy in Bristol, 1919-30', 160.
31 Skilleter, 'Housing Reform, Garden Suburbs…', 15.
32 Richard Coates, *The Street-Names of Shirehampton and Avonmouth* (Shirehampton: Shire Community Newspaper, 2011; rev.2013), 36: http://www.shire.org.uk/content/history/streetnames.pdf [accessed 28 March 2014].
33 Dave Backwith, *Housing not Herding? The Politics of Knowle West in the 1930s.* Unpublished thesis submitted for the degree of MA in Comparative Labour History, University of Warwick, 1990), 56.

Sea Mills Square with St Edyths Church.

the new Sea Mills estate, with a surprising beauty showing off in the evening sunlight. And vistas of trees and fields and pleasant cottages that the magic estate has managed to create.[34]

The history and context of the present development at Sea Mills has been thoroughly researched by John Roberts on behalf of the campaign to protect the area's garden suburb status in association with the Sea Mills and Coombe Dingle Community Project.[35] Roberts contextualises the Sea Mills Garden Suburb as a part of the coordinated post-war building boom, following the publication of the Tudor Walters Report of 1918. This report was produced by a committee which included Raymond Unwin, the architect and planner who did much to put garden-city and garden-suburb ideas into practice before the war. The national mood of post-War reconstruction ensured more state involvement in the enterprise. This fact was underlined by the presence of the President of the Lo-

34 Quoted in 'Bristol Homes Still an Inspiration', *Bristol Post* (16 September 2009): http://www.bristolpost.co.uk/Bristol-homes-inspiration/story-11281002-detail/story.html [accessed 10 April 2014].

35 John Roberts, *The Definition and Characteristics of a Post-WWI Garden Suburb with Particular Reference to Sea Mills Garden Suburb, Bristol: A Study by Save Sea Mills Garden Suburb in association with Sea Mills and Coombe Dingle Community Project* (Bristol: Save Sea Mills Garden Suburb/Sea Mills and Coombe Dingle Community Project, 2007).

cal Government Board, Christopher Addison, who dug the first shovelful of sod at Sea Mills in 1919, making it integral to the national housing scheme.[36] By 1931 the plans were literally made concrete in a large geometrical development of 1279 houses, covering the substantial area of today's Sea Mills (previously a small outlying settlement dating back to the Roman port of Abonae).

C. F. W. Dening drew up the master plan for Sea Mills, while George Oatley designed St Edyth's Church (1926-28) and the Methodist Church (1930) in the centre of the development.[37] The involvement of George Oatley, one of the directors of the limited company set up to found the Bristol Garden Suburb in Shirehampton in 1908, establishes a direct link between these neighbouring projects.[38]

Many of the houses at Sea Mills were constructed using relatively experimental techniques involving concrete building materials; the Parkinson PRC (Pre-stressed Reinforced Concrete) and 'Dorlonco' dwellings. The use of Parkinson concrete and Dorman Long steel-frame by builders William Cowlin and Son (Francis Nicholas Cowlin of this firm was also a director of the Shirehampton scheme) was piloted at the time as an innovative attempt to provide robust housing that could be quickly constructed. Eventually, however, these materials proved vulnerable to deterioration due to so-called 'concrete cancer'. It became apparent that, over time, the concrete became susceptible to water penetration which in turn led to the corrosion of the supporting steel framework. It now appears, however, that Bristol City Council's initial assessment of the long-term damage to the concrete houses at Sea Mills was unduly pessimistic. Subsequently a programme of patching and overcladding of the affected materials and other refurbishment has temporarily addressed such deterioration, providing a solution that is anticipated to mitigate the problem for at least

36 Roberts, *Definition and Characteristics of a Post-WWI Garden Suburb*, p. 18 and p. 40.
37 T.R. Wallis, *Sea Mills and the Battle of the Styles: Stylistic Variety in the Architecture of an Inter-War Garden Suburb and its Origins in Victorian Revivalism* (Bristol: T. R Wallis, 2004), 13. Keith Mallory also cites Benjamin Wakefield as the most likely designer of the Sea Mills project. Keith Mallory, *The Bristol House* (Bristol: Redcliffe Press in assoc. with Hoddell Pritchard, 1985), 69.
38 In Bristol George Oatley was to become most renowned as the principal architect of University of Bristol's Wills Building.

thirty years.[39] Therefore, while 132 of the Parkinson houses at Sea Mills were demolished during the 1980s, it was reported in 2011 that:

> A survey of the remaining Council-owned Parkinsons in Sea Mills, 2009/10, revealed there to be considerably less structural deterioration than had been anticipated in the 1980s. It is now known that all the Parkinsons are repairable, an extensive programme of repair by the City Council is immanent (246 in total).[40]

At the time of writing in 2014, this programme of house repair is near completion.

While the use of Parkinson PRC and 'Dorlonco' templates resulted in a majority of homes that are less 'cottagey' in their design and appearance than their neighbours in Passage Leaze, Shirehampton, the use of more conventional housing materials including traditional brick, brick and render, timber and slate accounts for some diversity in the Sea Mills estate as a whole. The recent report 'Sea Mills: Character Appraisal and Management Proposals' cites the involvement of four architectural firms in the design of the housing at Sea Mills: Benjamin Wakefield, W. H.Watkins, and Heathman & Blacker from Bristol and E.C.H. Maidman & W. A.Greener of Parkstone, in addition to the Council's architects.[41] This helped to ensure variety, while the grouping of house types helped to maintain overall compatibility of styles in the estate as a whole.

In many ways the radial pattern at Sea Mills, together with the inclusion of an abundance of features such as focal greens, avenues, culs-de-sac, in-

39 I am grateful to John Roberts for his technical explanation of the process of deterioration known as 'spalling'. He further commented that:

> Save Sea Mills Garden Suburb tried to persuade the Council to repair the houses more permanently using a method that had been successfully used on other PRC house types, but not yet tried on Parkinsons, with an estimated life-span of 60 years.

John Roberts, e-mail message to the author, 9 April 2014.
40 Bristol City Council, 'Sea Mills: Character Appraisal and Management Proposals', Conservation Area 21 (January 2011), 22: http://www.bristol.gov.uk/sites/default/files/assets/documents/sea-mills-character-appraisal.pdf [accessed online 26 March 2014].
41 Bristol City Council, 'Sea Mills: Character Appraisal and Management Proposals', 52.

tentionally designed views and glimpses and self-contained development, epitomises the garden-suburb idea more than any other location in Bristol. The idea that each home should have a garden with either an apple or cherry tree was an appetising foretaste of the desire to create edible cities on the part of twenty-first century permaculturalists. The inclusion of facilities such as allotments, a library, local shops, grounds for sport and play, and churches also meant that the garden-suburb objective to create a well serviced and self-sufficient community was met in a way that was not fulfilled elsewhere in the city's inter-war developments. Furthermore, there were plans for light industry at Sea Mills, which, had they happened, would have contributed towards the kind of local economic resilience that was key to Ebenezer Howard's original garden-city objectives and aspirations. John Roberts commented:

> Dening's original plan for Sea Mills included space 'reserved for industrial development' alongside the Avon, and a separate space reserved for small holdings, although neither space was eventually used for the purpose proposed. Together with the existing railway station, the intention seemed to be to make Sea Mills Garden Suburb as self-sufficient (or, in modern terms, sustainable) as possible.[42]

Bristol City Council first designated part of Sea Mills as a 'Conservation Area' in 1981.[43] This, however, has not always allayed concerns about threats to the character of the Sea Mills estate. A campaign group, 'Save Sea Mills Garden Suburb', was set up which successfully fought Bristol City Council proposals for the demolition and compulsory redevelopment of at least a fifth of the original housing which they feared would have significantly downgraded the character of the Conservation Area. It was estimated in a Town and Country Planning report of 2008 that 20% of the Parkinson concrete dwellings in particular were prone to defects, and, at that time, the scale of redevelopment looked to be even more extensive than this proportion.[44]

42 John Roberts, e-mail message to the author, 9 April 2014.
43 Bristol City Council, 'Sea Mills: Character Appraisal and Management Proposals', 7.
44 Town and Country Planning Association, *Garden City Settlements and Their Future: A Project Log*, TPCA website < http://www.tcpa.org.uk/downloads/20081031-GCS_Project_Log. doc > [accessed online 7 Dec 2008], 76.

From the outset of the development, an agreement between Philip Napier Miles, the owner of the land, and Bristol Corporation afforded some legal protection for the estate at Sea Mills into perpetuity. This agreement took the form of the so-called 'Napier Miles Covenants' 1919-1921, which stipulate 'That no part of the said lands and hereditaments hereby conveyed shall be used for any purpose other than that of a Garden Suburb'.[45] In 2007, however, Bristol City Council's Legal Team were exploring options to facilitate potential redevelopment and took on expensive additional legal advice since, ominously, they were 'working on whether the Covenant can be modified or removed'.[46]

Since the first edition of this pamphlet in 2008, proactive research and assessment by members of Save Sea Mills Garden Suburb and subsequent petitioning by residents appears to have been successful in making the case for the preservation of their estate's unique character. Indeed, in response to a petition of 1256 signatures, a large number for such a small place, the boundary of the Conservation Area was extended in 2008, to cover the entire garden suburb. This rectified the partial nature of the protection afforded by the 1981 designation. Bristol City Council produced a sympathetic report entitled 'Character Appraisal and Management Proposals' in 2011 which recognises the requirement to preserve the holistic integrity of the garden suburb's development and identifies the kind of alterations that would undermine its character.[47]

Save Sea Mills Garden Suburb continues to put pressure upon Bristol City Council to conserve the character and original vision of the estate in the light of the assessment of the 'Character Appraisal and Management Proposals' document. In 2014 they commented:

45 Roberts, *Definition and Characteristics of a Post-WWI Garden Suburb*, 3.
46 Alison Napper (Priority Stock Manager) to the PRC Project Consultation Group Meeting at the Council House, 26th September 2006. Bristol City Council website: http://www.bristol.gov.uk/ccm/cms-service/download/asset/?asset_id=17067004 [accessed 24 June 2007].
47 Bristol City Council, 'Sea Mills: Character Appraisal and Management Proposals'. The section on the Garden Suburb is largely based on Roberts's original analysis of the layout, and other extensive research by members of the Save Sea Mills Garden Suburb group.

Save Sea Mills Garden Suburb has been unsuccessful in persuading the Council to introduce an Article 4 Direction to control incremental changes to the appearance of the Conservation Area which usually do not require planning permission. Such changes, like the grubbing up of privet hedges and front gardens to provide hardstanding for cars, painting over red brick houses, or fitting out-of-character new windows, are, in the group's view, slowly leading to a death by a thousand cuts of the character and appearance of Sea Mills.

The group has also failed to prevent the immanent placement of a playground on one (or more) of the five greens that comprise the formal square at the heart of the Garden Suburb, known as Sea Mills Square. This will be highly detrimental to the character and appearance of the Conservation Area, in the group's view, and runs counter to the assessment in the Council's own Conservation Area Character Assessment and Management Proposals that: "Given its function as the centrepiece to the Garden Suburb, Sea Mills Square is particularly sensitive to change. Any change to its designed layout or formal character would be highly detrimental to the Conservation Area" (Sea Mills Conservation Area Character Assessment and Management Proposals, paragraph 8.30).[48]

Hillfields

Another location to be included in a survey of Bristol garden suburbs is the area around Maple Avenue and The Greenway in the Hillfields ward. Hillfields was the site of the city's first municipal housing constructed under the National Housing Scheme following the 1919 Addison Act, as can be still seen on the memorial plaque in Beecham Drive.[49] Under this legislation a funding model was set up by which costs were split three-

48 John Roberts e-mail message to the author 9 April 2014 (comment provided in conjunction with other members of the Save Sea Mills Garden Suburb group).
49 In a collection of reminiscences compiled by Jane Baker in 1988, Frederick Charles England recalled that the first houses in Beecham Drive 'were primarily to accommodate Belgian people who had been injured or left homeless in the Great War'. *Hillfields: The First Sixty Years A Local Study*, special edition for Fishponds Library Local History File, unpaginated.

way between central government, local authorities such as the Bristol Corporation and tenants.[50] This post-First World War development features some of the characteristics of the garden-city movement, such as relatively low-density housing set among green parkland and solidly designed houses. The houses at Maple Avenue were built in 1922 for the benefit of employees at the nearby E. S. and A. Robinson paper company,[51] a firm inspired by the non-conformist faith and paternalism of its Baptist founders Elisha Smith Robinson (a Liberal Lord Mayor of Bristol in 1866) and Alfred Robinson.[52] John Bartlett describes tenure arrangements under which houses 'could be purchased from the company by payments stopped from the workers' wage packets. As the Bristol Corporation owned the land, ground rents were paid directly to them'.[53] To this day Maple Avenue boasts a strikingly wide avenue lined with the still healthy maple trees, now venerable nonagenarians, which were specially imported from Canada as saplings. It retains plentiful green spaces above, towards Hillfields Avenue, and below, at Quadrant West. Such developments reflect the public demand to provide 'Homes Fit for Heroes' after the First World War – many war veterans moved into the newly constructed homes at Hillfields.[54] Despite poverty at Hillfields, the estate was regarded as a desirable place to live during the Interwar period, due to factors like its spirited sense of community and, in keeping with Sea Mills, the provision of gardens and green spaces. An older Hillfields resident spoke of such features fondly when recalling her childhood on the estate in the 1920s:

This was supposed to be one of the best council estates ever built and it was lovely because the builders put a tree in everybody's garden, you had an apple tree or a pear tree … at the time it was lovely. People had hedges, trees in their gardens, the trees up the road.[55]

50 Peter Malpass and Jennie Walmsley, *100 Years of Council Housing in Bristol* (Bristol: Faculty of the Built Environment, University of the West of England, 2005), 4.
51 http://en.wikipedia.org/wiki/Hillfields,_Bristol: [Accessed 15 Nov 2008].
52 http://www.benrff.org/documents/Philip%20Robinson.pdf: [accessed 15 Nov 2008].
53 John Bartlett, *Fishponds* (Stroud: Tempus, 2004), 126.
54 Paul Hoggett [*et al*], *Class, Race and Community Cohesion: A Profile of Hillfields, Bristol*. Report of research conducted for the Community Cohesion Unit of Bristol City Council by the University of the West of England and Community Resolve (Bristol: University of the West of England, 2008) [online]: http://www.uwe.ac.uk/hlss/research/cpss/research_reports/Hillfields.pdf [accessed 1 May 2014]. 6.
55 Hoggett [*et al*], *Class, Race and Community Cohesion*, 6.

However, while the layout and construction of the housing and generous open spaces may have been influenced by Howard's ideas, more far reaching aspects of his social and economic objectives were not carried through. Other parts of Hillfields continued to suffer from extreme poverty. Dresser documents claims of 'actual starvation' by members of a tenant's association in the ward in 1922 – any limited improvements were gains made due to tenant organisation and activism.[56] One of the key objectives of Howard's programme, that garden cities should be built on community-leased land, was not met. Occupancy has been determined by a combination of finance from private paternalism such as Robinson's, municipal control and later sells off to owner occupiers by 'right to buy' legislation. A survey found that 67% of homes in the Hillfields ward have owner occupation, while 19% are rented from Bristol City Council. Only 7% are rented from private landlords – the area is not considered a 'desirable' part of the property market, so few homes have fallen prey to 'buy to let' speculators.[57]

It is vital to remember that in Howard's vision a garden city encompassed not merely suburban houses with attractive gardens considered in isolation but an entire supporting economic and community infrastructure, rich in what today might be termed 'social capital'. When Hillfields was first developed, a tenant's association called the Hillfields Park Community Association campaigned hard for facilities and public spaces because, it was reported, 'there were no corner public houses, no theatres or cinemas, in fact no public meeting place at all apart from the local Baptist chapel'.[58] The situation was to persist for many years during which the school at Hillfields was used as a venue to host local events. After much lobbying the Community Association was finally granted some land for a Community Centre after the Second World War; but no funding to build it! The outcome was an impressive feat of community participation. In a section of a local history of the Hillfields estate compiled by Jane Baker it is recorded that:

56 See Dresser, 'Housing Policy in Bristol, 1919-30', 194 and 199.
57 Bristol City Council, *Hillfields: 2006 Ward Profile*, accessed online at: http://www.bristol.gov.uk/WardFinder/pdfs/hillfields-profile.pdf [accessed 20 October 2014], 11.
58 *Hillfields: The First Sixty Years A Local Study*, special edition for Fishponds Library Local History File, unpaginated.

Maple Avenue, Hillfields.

It had been decided that the centre would be built by voluntary labour, a remarkable decision, and Hillfields is the only Community Centre in the country to enjoy the distinction of having been built by the people who were to use it. While the men laboured at digging the foundations the wives were no less active providing teas and lunch and much encouragement. Work started out in 1950 on the site and over 40 men were involved in carrying out the necessary work.[59]

In most working-class suburbs non-profit making community ventures and amenities have fared poorly in recent decades. In Hillfields, for example, Beeching's axe severed Staple Hill Railway Station in 1966, Robin-

59 *Hillfields: The First Sixty Years.* Unfortunately later newspaper cuttings record that the Community Centre closed during the late 1990s, after running into substantial debt and regular incidents of vandalism which inflicted extensive damage to the premises. The claim that this was the only self-built community centre in the country may not be tenable as Lockleaze could also boast a self-built community centre constructed in the aftermath of the Second World War.

son's factory closed in 1996 and the local swimming pool and community centre have also been lost.[60] Without genuine community control and
ownership local facilities have proved to be vulnerable to council cuts or
sell-off and privatisation. Too often such areas have suffered from trick-
le-up economics in which 'wealth creation' and economic growth have
increased alongside an erosion of local amenities. Bristol City Council's
halt to support for the Woodland Way garden development has caused
controversy strongly relevant to the area's garden-suburb past. Local vol-
unteers and young offenders on community service orders transformed
a small area of disused land into a community nature reserve which was
to be used as a sensory garden for disabled children. Early in 2008 the
voluntary groups that had established the site, the Fishponds Locality
Action Group and Hillfields Futures, were unexpectedly given notice to
quit so that a social housing development could take place.[61] Such policy
shifts fuel the suspicion that environmental initiatives in working-class
districts are less valued than those in more prosperous neighbourhoods.

Speedwell

Near to Hillfields a direct labour scheme was used to construct a further 170 council houses at Ridgeway Road, Fishponds in the early
1930s.[62] Also between the Hillfields Ward and St George Ward is the
former mining area known as Speedwell where a separate municipal
housing estate was constructed on a 33 acre site between 1924 and
1931. Speedwell Estate has retained its identity as an inter-war housing
estate to this day with characteristic culs-de-sac, privet hedges and a
mix of gabled and non-gabled houses in the area around Selby Road
and Meadow Vale that counters the homogenous appearance of many
developments from this era. The gross density of 10.30 houses per acre
is comfortably in keeping with the Tudor Walters recommendation that
there should be twelve houses per acre.[63] The area was enhanced by

60 Hoggett [*et al*]., *Class, Race and Community Cohesion*, 4.
61 'Homes Blow for Sensory Garden Site', *Bristol Evening Post* 8 February 2008, 7. See also
Hoggett [*et al*]., *Class, Race and Community Cohesion*, 10.
62 John Lyes, *Bristol 1927-1933* (Bristol: Bristol Branch of the Historical Association, 2004), 9.
63 Rosamond Jevons and John Madge, *Housing Estates: A Study of Bristol Corporation Policy
and Practice Between the Wars* (Bristol: Pub. for the University of Bristol by J. A. Arrowsmith,
1946), 17.

the art-deco style Speedwell Baths nearby. This pool was funded by the Bristol Corporation and opened in 1937 and is now sadly missed following its closure in 2005.

Knowle West

By far the largest of the post-War municipal housing estates was developed at Knowle West and Bedminster from 1920 to 1939 numbering more than 6, 000 houses, together with a further 442 at nearby Bedminster Down.[64] The Knowle West development is a textbook example of a garden-suburb approach, in its most diluted sense, being lost in a massive housing programme. As Rosamond Jevons and John Madge noted, by 1939 Knowle West, with a population of 27, 000, was twice the size of Welwyn Garden City.[65] Many of the sociological and demographic facts we have about Bristol's inter-war housing estates are due to Jevons and Madge's detailed survey of the estates from the 1940s, published as *Housing Estates* (1946) – we know the occupations of the residents, how they travelled to work and what was for sale in the local shops. Again like the developments at Sea Mills and Hillfields, Knowle West was a part of the 1920s housing boom that followed the passage of the *Housing and Town*

Filwood Broadway, Knowle West.

64 Jevons and Madge, *Housing Estates*, 17.
65 Jevons and Madge, *Housing Estates*, 20.

Planning Act 1919 (the 'Addison Act') and the first Labour government's *Housing (Financial Provisions) Act 1924* (the 'Wheatley Act').

By the mid-1930s there was already considerable demoralisation and discontent at Knowle West, so much so that the local authorities attempted, unsuccessfully, to re-brand it as 'Filwood Park'.[66] Dissatisfaction with the solid new housing on the purpose-built estate perplexed middle-class support workers such as May Bolt, an 'Almoner at the Bristol Homeoepathic [*sic*] Hospital'. Bolt, who moved onto the estate as a warden in 1936 and had a great affection for the Knowle Westers, wrote:

> When I visited some of them and saw the pleasant little houses with the wide streets and the gardens and compared them with the awful slums of my other visits, I marvelled at the contrast and at the discontent.[67]

While some of the initial lack of facilities and services started to be addressed during the late 1930s onwards, progress was stopped by the outbreak of the Second World War. There was a sense that the mass programme of rehousing lacked opportunities for positive community relations to evolve and for neighbourhoods to bond. The geographical isolation from the rest of the city was an important factor, as Martin J. Powell argued, although partly mitigated by bicycles:

> Many of the men in the slums were on casual work. – 15 per cent on the new estates earned their living in this way. It was harder for these men now they were further away from the city centre and the docks. People who had previously lived by such things as hawking for furniture removal work in the new central area now found it impossible on the outskirts and the resentment built up.[68]

66 Martin J. Powell, 'From Bemmy Down to Bishopsworth', 103-122 in James Belsey *et al*, *Bristol: The Growing City: Life in the Suburbs – from the 18th Century to Today* (Bristol: Redcliffe, 1986), 110.
67 Unpublished, hand-typed account by Mary Bolt (warden 1936-1947) and Phyllis Bazeley (warden 1950-1960), *The Story of Corner Cottage Settlement. Knowle West 1936-1961* [1961?] (Bristol Central Library manuscript 08041199), 1.
68 Powell, 'From Bemmy Down to Bishopsworth', 112.

Filwood Broadway Cinema, Knowle West.

The story of Knowle West is largely one of unfulfilled promise – Filwood Broadway, for example, was intended to be a 'fine boulevard well lighted and lined with trees.'[69] It would be difficult to disagree with Dave Backwith's assessment that, while there were marked health benefits following slum clearance in the area, the improvement of the environment and the provision of lower-density housing, 'generally the houses and their gardens were seen as the most, if not the only positive feature of the estate'.[70] Madge Dresser may be justifiably sceptical about the popularity of gardens among low-income workers employed in manual labour, suspecting that gardening was partly imposed by municipal overseers as a means to make tenants more virtuous. However, other evidence suggests that a vast new urban population had voluntarily taken to vegetable gardening during the lean post-War years when there were well over a million allotment holders.[71] Certainly since at least the time of William Cobbett's *The English Gardener* (1829) there has been support for the working-class garden as a space that created opportunities to supplement diet, provide recreation, enjoy hobbies and socialise. Surveys carried out by Jevons and

69 Backwith, *Housing not Herding?*, 85.
70 Backwith, *Housing not Herding?*, 79.
71 Dresser, 'Housing Policy in Bristol, 1919-30', 207. David Crouch and Colin Ward, *The Allotment: Its Landscape and Culture* [1988], (Nottingham: Mushroom, 1994), 71-76.

Madge found that the residents were attracted to the 'pleasures of a new home with a garden, of the fresh and healthy atmosphere of the estate' which were chief among the compensations of living on the new schemes – two thirds of families interviewed were 'either very pleased or quite satisfied with the environment on the estates'– and claim that 'the great majority of gardens admirably reflect the care taken of them.'[72]

Unfortunately, even such infrastructure and services that did exist were lost towards the end of the Twentieth Century. The pool at Filwood Broadway which opened in 1962 was a victim of the same cuts to swimming pools as Speedwell, closing in 2005. Most symbolic, however, is the sad spectacle of the Broadway cinema in Filwood Park, opened in 1938 and once a cultural hub as it hosted not only film but concerts, boxing and bingo, but now boarded up for the last quarter of a century.[73]

Southmead

The slightly later Bristol Corporation estate started at Southmead at the end of the 1920s was one of the larger developments with up to a thousand houses built between the wars on land purchased by the Housing Committee in 1928.[74] By the time the initial Southmead and Knowle West schemes were completed after the war, Jevons and Madge estimated that around a third of all working-class Bristolian children lived on the Corporation estates. They also claimed that of these, 28% of under 14 year-olds lived in poverty (7% more than the city average).[75]

Similarly to Knowle West, the development at Southmead was used to re-house many families following slum clearance. The distance from the city centre meant that isolation and lack of opportunities often contributed

72 Jevons and Madge, Housing Estates, 66-67 and 78.
73 Dave Stephenson and Jill Willmott, *Bristol Cinemas* (Stroud: Tempus Publishing, 2005), 17. At the time of writing Bristol City Council hope to tempt a large supermarket chain to develop the building while maintaining the 'Metroland'-style façade. See City Design Group, Neighbourhoods and City Development, Bristol City Council, *Filwood Broadway Framework: Final Report* (Bristol: Bristol City Council, 2012), 10 and 21: http://www.bristol.gov.uk/sites/default/files/documents/planning_and_building_regulations/urban_design/urban_design_projects/Filwood%20Broadway%20Framework%20Final_1.pdf [accessed 21 April 2014].
74 Lyes, *Bristol 1927-1933*, 7.
75 Jevons and Madge, *Housing Estates*, 31-32.

Trowbridge Road, Southmead.

to continued deprivation on the new estate.[76] Therefore, also in common with Knowle West, some residents considered the supply of well constructed and spacious houses with gardens as a poor substitute for the kind of close knit neighbourhoods that they felt they had experienced previously. A further aggravating grievance was a sense that such redevelopments were something done *to* residents by municipal authorities for their own good without their participation in the decision-making process. In one Southmead resident's objection, the garden ironically signified a kind of uprooting:

76 Jevons and Madge, *Housing Estates*, 61.

I didn't ask to be moved from my so-called slum – it was nice there. The people were nice, always in and out. The rats didn't particularly bother us, either. Now what do I want with a garden and a box-hedge and all this respectability? Can you blame me for not caring? I want my comfortable slum, so I let the garden go.[77]

While as we have seen other residents of the Bristol's inter-war council estates often spoke of their gardens with pride and pleasure such contrasting comments indicate the complex and often contradictory expressions of community in such neighbourhoods. In this respect it is relevant that Jeremy Brent, a youth worker at Southmead for 25 years before his untimely death in 2006, based his analysis of the unstable and conflicting notions of the idea of 'community' on the estate at Southmead in his excellent study *Searching for Community*. Bristol City Council figures still identify parts of Southmead as among the 10% most deprived areas in England and Southmead Central as the most deprived area of the city for older people and in terms of income deprivation.[78]

Upper Horfield

Like Sea Mills, the estate at Upper Horfield made use of experimental housing using Parkinson pre-stressed reinforced concrete. The Upper Horfield scheme was a municipal housing estate, built 1926-1927 that has now been substantially redeveloped due to widespread structural damage caused by concrete cancer and damp which led to the demolition of the houses in 2005 (although as we have seen in the case of similar houses at Sea Mills, it is now known that such deterioration can be prevented and addressed by patching and overcladding). The abandonment of the more wholesome stone and clay bricks of earlier garden-suburb style dwellings denoted a shift from the Arts and Crafts tradition and is likely to have been motivated by factors that were pragmatic rather than aesthetic. Dresser records that a shortage of bricks after WWI was a consid-

77 Quoted in Roger Wilson, *Difficult Housing Estates* (London: Tavistock, 1963), 12. Brent, in *Searching for Community*, confirms that the Bristolian estate of Upfield described in Wilson's study is in fact based upon research undertaken in Southmead.
78 Bristol City Council, *Southmead: 2008 Ward Profile*: http://www.bristol.gov.uk/WardFinder/pdfs/southmead-profile.pdf [accessed online 18 Dec 2008], 8.

'Pride of Southmead', Southmead Youth Centre.

eration in the search for practical alternatives.[79] This said, developments could have been much worse. Backwith records the (rejected) proposal by Ernest Savory, the Conservative Chairman of the Housing Committee during the Interwar era for the construction of 1500 "'Chalets' made of corrugated iron and breeze blocks'.[80]

The regeneration scheme at Upper Horfield was completed in late 2008. The programme for mixed-tenure housing has, predictably, been developed with the higher density of 1,000 units (half of which are to be 'affordable') replacing the 600 homes on the former garden-suburb influenced estate.[81] The following comment from a correspondent who calls him or herself 'Sea Mills gardener' indicates that Bristolians that are affected by such redevelopment are aware of their garden-suburb heritage and the links between districts:

79 Dresser, 'Housing Policy in Bristol, 1919-30', 188.
80 Backwith, *Housing not Herding?*, 56-59.
81 Bristol Community Housing Foundation report, 'Regeneration of Upper Horfield Estate, Bristol', accessed online at: <http://www.southwesthousing.co.uk/pdfs/SWHI%20BP%20 Regeneration%20of%20Upper%20Horfield%20Estate.pdf> [accessed 7 Dec 2008], 1-2.

If the Council's recent development at Horfield is anything to go by, 'Sea' Mills will be a 'sea' of tarmac and flesh-pink concrete brickettes, instead of a 'sea' of the flowers, garden produce and tree-lined avenues we love to live with'.[82]

So far the verdict on the future of the Upper Horfield estate has been more upbeat for most tenants who are pleased to have escaped the increasingly dilapidated concrete housing. Nevertheless, in an essay published in 2010, lecturers on the built environment Henry Shaftoe and Andrew Tallon had already noted the apparent trend for property speculators to buy up the houses which they describe as 'fairly bland in design', for rent.[83]

As well as patterns of tenure, future conditions will be determined by the quality of local amenities and opportunities, conspicuous by their absence on many of Bristol's inter-war corporation estates. Dresser details the lack of social provision and the failure of coordination in terms of basic infrastructure such as transport, medical facilities, electricity and telephones. In Horfield, for example, a school, library and pub were only available at the end of the 1920s, several years after the housing was constructed. There was still no evidence of shops, a crèche, surgery, churches, social centres, sports grounds or a cinema by 1930.[84]

St Anne's

The council estate at St Anne's, built between 1928 and 1933 was similarly a product of the 1919 Housing Act and its successors during the early 1920s. Again the houses were well designed and laid out, under the coordinating eye of C. F. W. Dening.[85] Several streets in the development

82 Letter to *The Community Voice: Newsletter of the Sea Mills and Coombe Dingle Community Project* (2006), accessed online at: <http://community-voice.org.uk/cvoice/cvoice_21_5.pdf> [accessed 16 Nov 2008]. 5.

83 Henry Shaftoe and Andrew Tallon, 'Bristol: Not a Design-Led Urban Renaissance', 115- 131 in *Urban Design and the British Urban Renaissance*, ed. by John Punter (London: Routledge, 2010), 124.

84 Dresser, 'Housing Policy in Bristol, 1919-30', 194-196.

85 I am grateful to Andy Foyle, architectural historian and member of the Brislington Conservation and History Society who lives in the Brislington / St Anne's ward, for information about this development. Andy Foyle, e-mail message to the author, 16 December 2008.

are named after cathedrals, including Ripon Road (1928-33), Guildford Road (1928-33), St David's Crescent (1928) and Lichfield Road 1930-31), this ecclesiastical theme intriguingly being underpinned by their layout in a circled cross.[86] Within this circular development, inset with smaller culs-de-sac, many of the houses have characteristically prominent gables. While the homes were built with more traditional materials, and have proved to be more durable than the estate at Upper Horfield, in common with other Bristol Corporation schemes there is a lack of social amenities, exacerbated by the loss of St Anne's Park Station in 1970.

Lockleaze

The Bristol Corporation council housing at Lockleaze in north Bristol, although conceived during the Interwar period, was built later than the city's other garden-suburb inspired estates, not being developed until 1946-50, and marking perhaps the final episode in a four decade experiment. Noting that some of the first residents of the large new estate (numbering 1, 164 houses) had lost their former homes during the Blitz, Gerry Brookes writes of Lockleaze that:

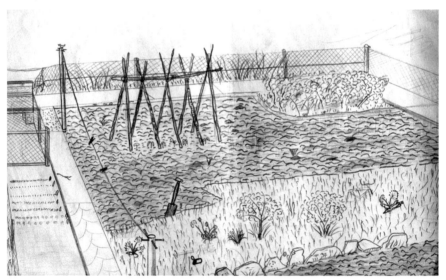

View of rear garden 4 Haydon Gardens, Lockleaze, 1961.

86 See *Terrier of Housing Estates*, Bristol Record Office 42098/1, 368-389.

The rather utopian idea was to create a garden suburb – a spacious, modern, self-sustaining place for all ages with its own schools, shops and recreation areas.[87]

Ian Haddrell describes the construction of the Lockleaze estate:

The original material palette used in Lockleaze comprised a simple set of complimentary [sic] materials. These generally included a mixture of rendered

concrete and precast sections and red/brown concrete tiles, or brown brickwork and brown concrete roof tiles.[88]

Regularly cycling down Romney Avenue in the present day I see that in many cases brightly painted exterior walls render the distinctive flat-topped houses less monotone, that village green spaces have been retained and that arrays of recently installed solar panels indicate local attempts at environmental and economic sustainability. Haddrell further points out that the street nomenclature is entirely derived from the names of artists from the Romantic era and their neo-Romantic successors.[89] Consistent with recollections from other garden suburbs such as Hillfields and Upper Horfield, one-time Lockleaze resident Joyce Storey expressed her appreciation for the estate's prolific greenery:

[...] in the spring sunshine, the avenue was a delight with the misty-pink blossom of the newly planted Japanese cherry trees. The pastel pinks, greens and greys of the painted houses blended with the foliage and clustered blossom of these trees. Every so often along the avenue there were cul-de-sacs, in front of which were grassland play areas, which had been planted by the Council with young saplings that looked as though they had been retained from the original meadow.[90]

87 Gerry Brooke, 'Distinct lack of community a worrying reality in "lost" suburb', *Bristol Post* (29 November 2011).
88 Ian Haddrell, *Lockleaze Schools* (Stroud: History Press, 2008), 7.
89 Haddrell, *Lockleaze Schools*, 8-9.
90 Quoted by Haddrell, *Lockleaze Schools*, 7-8 from The House in South Road.

Despite this early promise, Lockleaze has shared some of the endemic problems of deprivation and lack of services with other Bristolian council estates. According to a 2008 Ward Profile for Lockleaze compiled by Bristol City Council, three Lockleaze wards are ranked as among the 10% most deprived areas in both Bristol and England.[91] Nevertheless the area has an established tradition of community activism with Lockleaze Voice and Lockleaze Environment Group campaigning to preserve something of the low-density character of the estate and opposing council sell-offs of green spaces.

Keynsham: Somerdale Garden Factory

Another significant example of the influence of the garden-city movement locally was at nearby Keynsham, where Fry's the Quaker chocolate manufacturers developed the 'Somerdale Garden Village' for their workers at the factory in 1925.[92] Quaker families such as Fry, Cadbury and Rowntree were prominent in chocolate manufacture and enjoyed a reputation for philanthropic attempts to raise the conditions of their workforce at production centres such as Bournville, New Earswick and Somerdale. As nonconformists, Quakers were excluded from public office in the government, church and military until the repeal of the Test and Corporation Acts in 1829. They often, therefore, found a professional outlet in business; chocolate production was particularly fitting given their affinity with the temperance movement.

The location of Somerdale on the banks of the River Avon at Keynsham Hams was chosen not only for its transport connections using rail, road and water but also for the ample development space and attractive surroundings. The site was carefully selected and it took nearly fifteen years to landscape and to construct the factory for production. The factory was named 'Somerdale' following a national competition in 1923. It was consciously planned with the inspiration of the garden-city movement. Peter Roberts of Keynsham Heritage Trust said Somerdale

91 Bristol City Council, *Lockleaze: 2008 Ward Profile* [Online]: https://www.bristol.gov.uk/WardFinder/pdfs/lockleaze-profile.pdf [accessed 30 April 2014].
92 Skilleter, 'Housing Reform, Garden Suburbs…', 18. Former employee Eric Miles produced a300-page photographic history of the factory's construction and operation on the eve of its closure – *Somerdale Story 1921 to 2009* (2009).

A souvenir tin from Somerdale. Date unknown.

was really in part conceived as 'a garden factory'.[93] This is confirmed by the inclusion of lines from the July 1928 edition of *The Quiver in the Fry's Works Magazine*:

> We have brought the people from the rural areas to the factories of the town: let us take back our industries to the wide spaces and purer air of the countryside: that way lies content and happiness.[94]

Such lines posit the idea that the industrial revolution could enter a new enlightened phase ushering a reconciliation of industrialism with Romanticism – the magazine is interspersed with quotes from William Wordsworth, John Keats and other Romantic-era poets, thus soothing age-old antagonisms between the country and the city that Raymond Williams documented, and solving both lack of rural opportunity and urban pollution.[95] In meeting the preconditions for human happiness, health and well-being the idealism of Fry's approach at Somerdale is far-reaching and chimes with a key aspect of Howard's programme to reconcile the town-country split by creating intentional communities without rural isolation or the squalor of city slums and heavy industry.

93 Personal conversation at 'Remembering Somerdale' event, 4 November 2008.
94 *Fry's Works Magazine 1728-1928* (Bi-Centenary Number) ed. by W. T. Pearce ([Bristol]: J. S. Fry & Sons Ltd, 1928), 67.
95 Raymond Williams. *The Country and the City* (London: Chatto & Windus, 1973).

Despite the pastoral elements in the Garden-Cities Movement, as Frederick Aalen points out, Howard's enthusiasm for the socially emancipatory potential of the latest technology distinguished his ideas from those that were 'harking back to a pre-industrial age'.[96]

The playing fields and other recreational facilities and the Fry Club and Conference Centre were a key part of the employee benefits on offer.[97] The housing estate adjacent to the factory was constructed during the mid-1920s along garden-suburb principles, with soundly built houses and immediately available employment for key factory employees – as well as permanently hanging with sickly sweet wafts of chocolate. The housing estate that was eventually built, however, was considerably smaller than that first projected. In an unpublished dissertation based upon Fry's internal publications, Tim Clench notes that only 64 of the initially projected 176 houses were completed and that a much larger programme to build up to 500 houses was shelved.[98]

Following the merger with Cadbury's in 1919 much of the paternalist ethos of the Fry family, who operated under the motto 'Happiness in Industry', was carried over to the new factory at Keynsham when production was shifted from central Bristol in 1935. A Fry's mission statement dating from this time stated the aim to give 'the workpeople the best facilities for recreation and happiness.'[99] In this respect a tension arises between the liberal reformist aspirations of paternalist employers and the more radical objectives for social change that Ebenezer Howard and subsequent garden-city planners advocated. Despite the generosity of Fry and its reputation as a model employer, from the outset there had been a regime in which prayer and scripture were mandatory at work, while chat between women and men was prohibited and pubs were off limits even outside of working hours, both offences which numbered

96 Frederick H. A. Aalen, 'English Origins', pp. 28-51 in *The Garden City: Past, Present and Future*, ed. by Stephen V. Ward (London: E & FN Spon, 1992), 32.
97 The Fry Club and facilities remain in operation in 2014, despite the closure of the Cadbury factory.
98 Tim Clench, 'Happiness in Industry' – Working for J. S. Fry & Sons, Cocoa and Chocolate Manufacturers, Bristol (1865-1971) [Unpublished Final Project Report for Open University course DA301 2001], 7.
99 Quoted by Paul Chrystal, *Cadbury and Fry Through Time* (Stroud: Amberley Publishing, 2012), 20.

The Fry's factory, Somerdale. Date unknown.

among misdemeanours which could result in financial penalties or dismissal.[100] At Fry's female workers had been known as 'angels' and male workers as 'devils'. A former resident from Greenbank, site of the former Packer's chocolate factory (later Elizabeth Shaw) also told me that her mother quipped about 'Fry's angels and Packer's devils', to point up the contrast in attitudes towards local employers on the part of their workers. At Fry's employees were expected to be 'clean, sober and of good character' and stoppages and wage deductions could be made for talking on the shop floor.[101]

When Fry's became a subsidiary of Cadbury's, Somerdale employees continued to be rewarded with a package of benefits including hospital funds, pensions, sick benefits that were generous given the economic climate in the years following the Depression. Despite the inherent tedium involved in producing standardised confectionary on production lines with a rigid division of labour, many young working-class people aspired to work in

100 Chrystal, *Cadbury and Fry,* 22-23.
101 According to interviewee in 1978 BBC documentary on Somerdale presented by Gwyn Richards.

the factory to take advantage of the preferred working conditions on offer. Women outnumbered men by a ratio of 2:1. Even after the War, if they lacked qualifications they might demonstrate good character by taking along their Sunday school book and an example of some embroidery. Given this continuation of the old Fry's paternalism, there was very little agency for workers within Somerdale although industrial disputes were not unknown, later in the Twentieth Century. Shop- floor activism during the 1930s finally made some inroads into the entrenched paternalism. At this time Ernest Bevin, then General Secretary of the Transport and General Workers' Union, negotiated a deal with Egbert Cadbury to recognise trade union representation at the garden factory.

Mostly however, worker loyalty to the amenities at Somerdale was maintained, as was reflected in the high-profile and spirited fight to save the plant, then run by Cadburys, when its phased closure was announced in October 2007.[102] Film director Ken Loach joined a protest march against the relocation of production to Poland to save labour costs. The tensions between the tradition of paternalism at the site and the imperative to turn increasing profits were longstanding. Somerdale's precarious situation was revealed in Cadbury's announcement that confirmed the company's intention to close the Keynsham factory by 2010, despite continued profit making and the fact that most of the production at the site is for the home market. The economic conflict of interests between confectionary workers and their bosses could only be partially glossed over by the aspiration to 'Happiness in Industry' and has perhaps sharpened the sense of betrayal at Cadbury's imminent relocation. Decades of rationalisation and job losses from the 1960s onwards seem to have only delayed the perhaps inevitable capitulation to the operations of the global market.

This sense of betrayal was to be sharpened when the giant American food producer Kraft bought out Cadbury in a hostile takeover in 2010. The predatory corporation's promises to reconsider and save the Somerdale factory were swiftly broken; renewed hope for the remaining 400 workers was dashed when Kraft reneged on its promises – within a week of

102 Campaign website: http://wwwsaveoursomerdale.co.uk/ [accessed 22 Jan 2008, now unavailable].

46

Fry's chocolate factory in 1928.

its takeover![103] The factory closed on 31st March 2011. At the time of writing in 2014 work has started on demolishing the garden factory and volume-house builders Taylor Wimpey have been granted planning permission to build up to 700 houses and accompanying development on the site.[104]

Real Reform?

Those influenced by Ebenezer Howard's ideas sought to accommodate housing schemes within state capitalist or private industrial enterprises. Inevitably, obstacles confronted his *Peaceful Path to Real Reform* when attempting to transform the conditions of working-class communities within a capitalist infrastructure. Fundamental conflicts of interest between the need for a residential community to flourish in an environment with well designed architecture, pleasant surroundings, adjacent social amenities and the means to make a living were not easily reconciled with the demand to balance budgets and accumulate profits. Such tensions were to become particularly pronounced during the Interwar period as the different aspirations of capitalist sponsors and those like Raymond Unwin, a leading architect of garden cities and suburbs, who looked to the uplifting and progressive aspects of the projects. Working in the tra-

103 'Kraft job row earns firm a city rebuke', *The Bristol Post* (27 May 2010), 3.
104 'Permission for 770 homes on old Cadbury's site', *The Bristol Post* (28 February 2014), 16.

dition of William Morris, Unwin sought to transform the quality of human life by beautifying surroundings. Mark Swenarton writes:

> For socialists such as Raymond Unwin, the garden city movement was the way to make an unparalleled improvement in the lives of the people; for capitalists such as Lever, it offered a way of making the workforce more contented (and thereby more productive) without affecting the basic relationships of capitalist production.[105]

Employers hoped that satisfying employees' basic needs would help to nurture a quiescent workforce while local government housing and planning administrators believed that the provision of municipal housing could head off the potential for revolutionary aspirations, as the mass demand for decent homes helped to fuel labour militancy after the First World War. However, the provision of the inter-war municipal housing schemes influenced by the garden-city movement coincided with the turbulent years of the General Strike, the Depression and the Hungry Thirties. This created an environment in which the chief imperative was to be cost effective. The result was a dilution of quality in municipal housing, due to pecuniary incentives on the part of local authorities operating in the context of an economic downturn, and understandable pressure from slum dwellers, homeless families and others on waiting lists who were desperate for housing sooner rather than later.[106] While the low density of twelve houses per acre under the 1924 Housing Act was adhered to, Jevons and Madge regarded the higher percentage of the more ample houses with parlours built immediately after the war as a critical difference to the non-parlour houses of later municipal developments.[107]

Furthermore, Swenarton convincingly argues that Raymond Unwin and Alexander Harvey (the chief architect at Bournville) were also

105 Mark Swenarton. *Homes Fit for Heroes: The Politics and Architecture of Early State Housing in Britain* (London: Heinemann Educational, 1981), 6-7.
106 In the mid-1930s the health department conducted about 1,400 housing inspections annually, with a yearly average of 980 houses found unfit for habitation,' *City and county of Bristol Annual Report of the Medical Officer of Health, Bristol: 1934–1938.* passim. Findings reported by Martin Gorky, 'Public Health in Interwar England and Wales: Did it fail?', *Dynamis* 28 (2008) Section 4.
107 Jevons and Madge, *Housing Estates*, 20-21.

eventually complicit in taking an approach to up scaling projects from small model villages to large council estates that prioritised the 'simplification of design and the standardisation of building components'.[108] This was rational enough given the demands of the moment and the incentive to make economies of scale, but was to lead inexorably to the stultifying conformity and monotony of later twentieth-century housing schemes, in which aesthetic priorities came a poor second to budgetary considerations. A report on Bristol's Southmead estate, for example, speaks of the 'monotonous consistency of building type and streetscape which emphasizes its separation from surrounding areas'.[109] As we have also seen in Bristol, the scale – though not the quality – of garden-city influenced planning exceeded that of its 'official' representation in Letchworth and Welwyn Garden City. The history of Bristolian inter-war planning in the 1920s and 1930s, as told in studies such as those by Dresser and Backwith, is one of deteriorating standards, with economies in the quality of housing construction and increasing standardisation of design.[110] This was accompanied by cost cutting in the provision of public amenities and community infrastructure. Commenting on the pitiful absence of amenities at Knowle West and throughout the municipal housing estates of Bristol's working-class suburbs, Backwith writes:

This situation flowed from the Post-War Government's conception of municipal housing which, despite the inspiration of the Garden City movement, was of housing estates rather than integrated, 'reconstructed' communities. Given the numbers of houses promised in the 'Homes fit for Heroes' rhetoric it seems, with hindsight, an amazing oversight that the need to furnish estates with the social institutions which were essential, if taken for granted, part of the working class life was simply not considered.[111]

108 Swenarton, *Homes Fit for Heroes*, 24.
109 Safe Neighbourhoods Unit, *The Southmead Survey 1991* (Bristol: Bristol City Council / Bristol Safer Cities Project, 1991), 3; Quoted in Jeremy Brent, *Searching for Community: Representation, Power and Action on an Urban Estate* (Bristol: Policy Press, 2009), 77.
110 Dresser, 'Housing Policy in Bristol, 1919-30', 191.
111 Backwith, *Housing not Herding?*, 124.

The result was that few vestiges of the garden-city movement survived into the brave new world of Bristol's post-War reconstruction from the late 1940s onwards. Planning influenced by the Tudor Walters report emerged because of concerns about the poor quality of working-class housing; garden-city principles that had been extremely diluted by the outbreak of the Second World War were effectively lost altogether in the tower block housing that was to follow. This was partly explained by the even more onerous demands of reconstruction facing post-War administrations in the aftermath of the Blitz. It should also be remembered that many lives were lost and much housing stock was destroyed in the garden-suburbs influenced municipal estates, particularly at Horfield and Southmead due to their proximity to the Bristol Aeroplane Company at Filton, but casualties were also recorded in all of the city's municipal council estates.[112]

There was also a radical contrast in the defining ethos of the kind of modernism influenced by Le Corbusier, whose conception of houses as machines for living in came to predominate in many more urban schemes after 1945. As I have shown, under the inspiration of Howard, English town planning had been imbued with garden-city ideas – the Town and Country Planning Association began life as the Garden Cities Association at the end of the Nineteenth Century. Howard had a holistic vision of planning in which there were several key elements that helped to define the garden-city project – strong housing design creating dwellings that are durable, comfortable and aesthetically appealing; a rejection of urban sprawl so homes are situated in environmentally attractive surroundings which have accompanying gardens, green spaces nearby and are free from pollution; a variety of social amenities to encourage community cohesion and avoid alienation; opportunities for creative work within walking distance so that the gap between workplace and home is minimal. In this sense garden cities were in fact an antidote to today's leafy suburbia in their explicit rejection of the separation of work and home. The Edwardian idea of the garden city and garden suburb may enjoy a new relevance as critics posit the idea of an 'End of Suburbia' in the title of Gregory

112 'The Bristol & District Blitz War Memorial: A Register of those who Lost their Lives due to Enemy Action and Surrounding Districts, 1940-1944', compiled by John Penny: http://fishponds.org.uk/bristolmem.html [accessed 21 April 2014].

Sea Mills from the air in 1931.

Green's film documenting the social consequences of rapidly depleting oil reserves.[113] One of these consequences could be an end to the kind of urban developments in which the priorities of through traffic by private cars have over-ridden the needs of local neighbourhoods.

Another radical ingredient of Howard's conception of the garden city was that the development should be community owned. Once the capital had been raised to plan and construct the infrastructure, homes should be leased from the community constituted as a democratic entity. Rather than mortgage payments or rent to a private owner or municipal authority a regular payment is made to a community fund, thus the intention was to build up a sense of direct responsibility for the locality on the part of the residents, and to create an alternative to interference and profiteering on the part of outside agencies whether state or private. Proponents of the garden-city idea went to considerable lengths to create stable communities in line with what nineteenth-century German sociologist Ferdinand Tönnies characterised as *Gemeinschaft*, a social structure based upon face-to-face communication, though without wishing to return to the more exclusive and static societies of a pre-industrial past.

113 *The End of Suburbia: Oil Depletion and the Collapse of the American Dream* (2004).

There was a conscious intention to implement environmental conditioning in this, through attempts to bring about the preconditions in which
mutual aid and self-help would flourish. Partly to this end culs-de-sac
were created such as those at Sea Mills so that microcommunities would
emerge, neighbours would be encouraged to cooperate and enjoy a degree
of collectivity rather than being divided by individualism. Some planners
were reluctant to incorporate hedges and fences as they presented physical
barriers between households. The environmental approach was associated
with early sociologists such as Seebohm Rowntree who was influential in
supporting model industrial villages, the experimental settlements that
were to be the forerunners of garden cities. Gillian Darley writes that
'with industrial interests [Seebohm Rowntree] placed particular emphasis
on root causes, recognising that change of environment was 100% more
worthwhile than charity meted out later; the model village versus the
dosshouse. He gave people independence and the best possible means
with which to achieve it'.[114]

The lack of pubs was motivated by concern for alcoholism's role in undermining social ties and perpetuating poverty. When straightedge punks
rejected alcohol as a dissipation of the social struggle, taking a different
approach from those among the first generation of punks who followed
The Sex Pistols into liberation through excess, they were taking part in
a dispute that had been familiar in countercultural circles for more than
a century. The reluctance to provide public houses in garden suburbs
was based on links between alcohol and poverty in studies by reform-
ing social thinkers such as Henry Mayhew, Charles Booth and Seebohm
Rowntree as much as a puritanical distaste for pleasure. However, while
there were established temperance leanings in the Chartist, co-operative
and labour movements, it was also recognised that in practice it was no-
toriously difficult to determine the extent to which alcohol was the cause
or effect of deprivation. Some socialist critics regarded temperance as
an attempt to blame disadvantaged individuals for systemic failures and
anticipated the futility of prohibition. Even a teetotaller such as Philip
Snowden wrote in 1908 that 'alcoholism cannot be completely solved
apart from the treatment of the whole problem of the economic and social condition of the people', noting the correlation with bad housing and

114 Darley, *Villages of Vision*, 188-189.

acknowledging that 'the public house has become the centre of social intercourse'.[115] Regardless of objections to alcohol consumption, public houses were (and obviously remain!) cherished public spaces and the lack of them on moral grounds was a thin excuse for the failure to provide social spaces – Jevons and Madge objected 'Why are there no billiard saloons or milk bars?'[116] The reason, it seems, was that the Housing Committee was extremely cautious about the presence of licensed premises on the new municipal estates. John Lyes records that in 1931 the Committee agreed that premises could only be opened if it could be demonstrated that a majority of tenants were in favour, although some members preferred an outright ban.[117] This nervousness on the part of local authorities may have been motivated by considerations beyond public health and order. Alison Ravetz suspected that the 'weakness of the public realm on estates, were disincentives to engage in union or political activity'.[118]

Garden-city advocates hoped to create a society of empowered citizens rather than simply consumers or employees. In this they anticipated key components of Murray Bookchin's creation of a reinvigorated *polis* which would incorporate the positive features of Athenian democracy – conviviality, direct democracy, creativity, ecologically sustainability, locally committed yet internationalist in its embrace through libertarian municipalism – and also present-day New Urbanist initiatives in the United States.[119] Jevons and Madge identified the lack of a culture of self-government and opportunities for direct democracy through community-run social centres on Bristol's municipal estates as a problem to be remedied back in the 1940s.[120]

115 Philip Snowden, *Socialism and the Drink Question* (London: Independent Labour Party, 1908), 3, 57-59 and 82.
116 Jevons and Madge, *Housing Estates*, 86.
117 Lyes, *Bristol 1927-1933*, 19.
118 Alison Ravetz, *Council Housing and Culture: The History of a Social Experiment* (London: Routledge, 2001), 167.
119 Discussed in works such as *From Urbanization to Cities: Towards a New Politics of Citizenship* [1992], rev. edn (London: Cassell, 1995).
120 Jevons and Madge, *Housing Estates*, 70. Backwith, however, demonstrates that the Knowle Westers could be far from politically apathetic when the need arose, citing the spirited rout of fascist blackshirts in Melvin Square, six weeks before the celebrated 'Battle of Cable Street' in 1936, *Housing Not Herding*, 98-99 and 137.

Howard did not, however, challenge the context of the vast inequality of wealth and hence power in which such social relationships already exist. A thoroughgoing improvement in human physical conditions and the physical environment is largely unobtainable in isolation from wider social and cultural transformation. Political questions of power and ownership will continue to provide challenges to contemporary initiatives like Transition Towns whose advocates will need to be 'savvy' and learn some hard historical lessons if their good intentions are not to be compromised by accommodating entrenched economic interests. The achievements at Letchworth and Welwyn Garden City were undoubtedly diluted as a consequence of the heavy reliance of the garden-city programme upon wealthy sponsors such as George Cadbury and William Lever for advice and financial backing.[121]

It seems to me that there are strong parallels here with the common accusation that has become almost cliché in discussions about the Arts and Crafts Movement – that finely crafted goods were produced at a cost that could only be afforded by the better off patrons. In any discussion about the Arts and Crafts Movement it is customary for detractors to point out that, 'Ah, such beautiful work, but for all their lofty principles, these socialist artists could only sell to the rich'. There is some truth in this. Yet, if it is ironic, it is not the crushing irony that it may seem. Socialists such as William Morris and Charles Robert Ashbee did not overlook the all-embracing reality of capitalism and the wealthy elite's grip upon the means of production, which they knew could not be simply sidestepped. It was their awareness that mass-production in factories had largely concentrated the control of the production in the hands of a few wealthy capitalists and exacerbated alienation of producers through the division of labour that prompted the Arts and Crafts approach. The principles and practice of the almost contemporaneous Arts and Crafts and the Garden-City Movements were sound ones which floundered on the massive inequalities of wealth and power in the society within which they found themselves. The practical consequences of this context were all too apparent. In Knowle West for example, tenants suffered from the damp despite new homes because they could not afford

121 Darley, *Villages of Vision*, 184.

to the heat the houses that they rented. [122] Howard maintained his commitment to far-reaching social change despite the conflicting demands and compromises that led to the curtailment and watering down of key aspects of his programme.

For the Garden-City Movement confidence that improved material circumstances could positively influence social outlooks and structures fed into a belief that that social gains could be made through benign planning and design, hence paving the way to ongoing transformation. Influential urban theorists such as Patrick Geddes later shared this environmentalist premise, in part derived from nineteenth-century thinkers such as John Ruskin and William Morris. The ecological imperatives of the great Austrian utopian artist and designer Friedensreich Hundertwasser were at once strikingly original yet strongly in this earlier Romantic tradition. His belief that all urban dwellers had an obligation to plant trees – a 'tree duty' – was part of a declaration that a revolutionary transformation towards a new urban mode of living was necessary in which planning and design should be assessed by its both its life-enhancing and aesthetic qualities and ecological consequences.

While the Garden-City Movement did not anticipate the radical environmental trajectory of Hundertwasser with his extravagant material constructions, it was characterised by prevailing planning assumptions about the well-being of individuals and communities that contrasted substantially with those that predominated after the Second World War. A functional, utilitarian approach began to emerge with demands for mass provision of municipal housing as quantitative measurements – the 'felicific calculus' of the greatest happiness of the greatest number – replaced more qualitative estimations of community well being. This is evident in the starkly contrasting, and contested, versions of modernity represented by the Garden City or made concrete in the tower block estates of the post-War era. One telling change of direction in the philosophy of well-being was brought about by the democratisation of private transport through mass production. In this way urban dwellers were held to benefit through the easy transit brought about by the ownership of affordable cars and their accompanying infrastructure. Strategic decisions

122 Backwith, *Housing not Herding?*, 80.

to prioritise the needs of the motor car as a progressive change too often over-rode the quality of life of localities such as Bristol's Baptist Mills and Eastville, severed by major roads. The potential for communities integrated with places of work becomes an impossible dream in such a context and has yet to be reversed by the predicted trend towards Internet home working. Garden-suburb planning also represents an optimistic view of the motivations and impulses of intended residents. This is clear from efforts to design in considerations of well-being, hoping to achieve a change in housing conditions with an improved physical and natural environment and aspirations to greater community autonomy, which would in turn bring about a change for the better in society. This was surely lost in planning strategies that presumed certain urban populations to be dysfunctional, an attitude which seemed to cause the authorities to regard inner-city populations primarily as a problem to be policed and contained by the time riots erupted in the city (including Southmead and Knowle West) during the 1980s.

As we learn from the popularity of psychogeography and its contribution to radical history in recent decades, attention to such phenomena as patterns of settlement, sites of celebration and struggle and ecology has the potential to transform our experience of moving through, and being in, a particular environment. Radical social history taking this approach not only reveals the glaring mismatch of the mansion and the tenement but also explores the perhaps more subtly contested versions of social and economic forces at play in the presence and governance of the sports ground, the allotment, the cinema and the pub. It aspires therefore to encourage understanding of the enduring paradigms of hierarchy and authoritarianism and their underlying mechanisms of social control as well as open up more clearly to the imagination possibilities for authentic transformation and liberation. Such an attunement calls for watchfulness not just of the attractive formalist characteristics of a garden-suburb house and garden which may be similar in Sea Mills, Knowle West or Speedwell, but the less tangible influences of capital flows and social power that determine the conditions of life alongside bricks and mortar.

I hope that this pamphlet has revealed the profound, yet now largely forgotten, influence of the garden-city movement in defining the urban morphology of the estates around Bristol's residential periphery. Today schemes closest to the garden-city influence, such as the early housing at Shirehampton, have endured and held their value more than more recent municipal housing or estates such as those at Knowle West and Southmead. On the one hand the inter-war municipal housing programme was relatively successful in the construction of 9, 000 dwellings by 1931 and 15, 000 in the Interwar period as a whole.[123] However the undoubted quantitative achievements in terms of bulk provision were not matched by qualitative improvements in community well-being. At the same time the vision and idealism of the Garden-City Movement was lost in a climate of economic expediency and, consequently, many of the areas loosely influenced by Howard's ideas through the Tudor Walters report are now deprived areas, such as Knowle West, Southmead, Hillfields and parts of Shirehampton. Passing through the city suburbs to arrive at Temple Meads Station from any direction today it is easy to imagine that the social and environmental legacy of the Twentieth Century could have been so much better.

Today

Peter Hall and Colin Ward argue that the mass production of the motor car and the post-War baby boom were both critical factors in undermining the possibility of a revival of the garden cities in the second half of the Twentieth Century.[124] This analysis has proved to be accurate, with the result that, despite a rhetorical revival in the use of the term 'garden city', presently proposed garden cities turn out to be blueprints for new town developments lacking many of the characteristics that inspired Ebenezer Howard and other pioneers of the idea more than a century before.

Garden suburbs were intended as developments to support what – according to prevailing Edwardian notions – were the deserving poor. In the long run however it was perhaps inevitable that, in more desirable areas, market forces would ensure that such homes would be unlikely

123 Dresser, 'Housing Policy in Bristol, 1919-30', 161. Jevons and Madge, *Housing Estates,* 9.
124 Peter Hall and Colin Ward, *Sociable Cities: The Legacy of Ebenezer Howard* (Chichester: Wiley, 1998), Chapter 7.

to stay affordable and would deprive even these sectors of the working class of the quality of design and spaciousness that they achieved. In the Hampstead Garden Suburb much surrounding woodland has long since been cut down and developed while the homes are the preserve of the super-rich – the larger houses currently being offered on the market for several million pounds. Murray Bookchin was right to observe that the central shortcoming in Howard's proposal for social change was that visionary design is only one element of the profound transformation that he sought. In his brave attempt to construct a bridge linking pragmatism and utopia, Bookchin suggests, Howard was to leave 'undefined the nature of work, the control of the means of production, the problem of distributing goods and services equitably, and conflicting social interests that collect around these issues' – in short the other materials of which community is forged.[125] Today's predominance of empty dwellings and office blocks, second homes and demographic factors such as a sharp-rise in single-occupancy households indicates that the housing shortage is as much about distortions in capital flows (locally and globally) and social power, expressed through the hugely inequitable distribution of land and housing, as the problem of a deficient supply of buildings.

A lot has happened since I wrote the first edition of this pamphlet back in 2008. In 2008 Gordon Brown (Prime Minister 2007-2010) proposed a series of new 'eco-towns' based on his admiration for the housing innovations he had seen on a visit to Hammarby Sjöstad in Sweden.[126] In June 2007 Housing Minister Yvette Cooper had announced that the Bristol area was to be the site of a test development, Hanham Hall, a pilot for Gordon Brown's plans to create five of these 'eco-towns', which were ultimately intended to house up to 100, 000 people in homes with zero-carbon emissions.[127] This development is now underway with some residents already living in the eco-village and completion scheduled for 2015. The final project will consist of around 180 homes, of which approximately a third will be designated as affordable while others will be shared ownership. This is undoubtedly a

125 Murray Bookchin, *The Limits of the City* (New York: Harper Colophon, 1974), 119.
126 'Brown "inspired" by Swedish eco-town', *Building Design* (1 June 2007), 5.
127 'Eco-villages challenge launch by minister', *Western Daily Press* (4 June 2007), 4.

useful experimental site with environmental features that are a significant advance on other estates by volume house builders. While this is to be welcomed it seems that we have to go back to the Garden-City Movement and its influence – albeit diluted – on the construction of inter-war estates, and post-War new towns, to look at what actually constitutes the collective provision of intentional community planning for social and environmental ends. A slow build movement that gets it right in terms of combining attractive design (a subjective quality of course!) with local distinctiveness and ecological innovation would surely in the long run be more effective in meeting human housing and economic needs than the perpetual regeneration of urban areas. This benefits today's corporate construction industry but does nothing for the social fabric of city life or the environment.

If there were limitations in the eco-villages of the Brown administration, divergence from the radical aspirations of the garden-city pioneers has become even more evident in the proposals of the succeeding government. When Brown's political opponents in the Conservative-Liberal coalition government gained power in 2010, the idea of a new generation of garden cities emerged and gained leverage in planning discussions once more. The right-wing think tank Policy Exchange saw them as a way for the construction industry to make profits in the context of a worsening housing crisis. It is also believed, however, that the Prime Minister David Cameron will approach such initiatives with caution, given that the demand would be chiefly in South-East England where available land is difficult to identify and where such proposals would risk stiff opposition from Tory-voting constituents in the Home Counties.[128]

At the time of writing in 2014, the coalition's Deputy Prime Minister Nick Clegg has announced the government's intention to initiate three new schemes explicitly called 'garden cities', of 15, 000 houses each.[129] There is currently no stated start date for these developments, which are major projects, although significantly smaller in scope than the Brown

128 Jonathan Brown, 'Cameron accused of dropping support for garden cities for fear of a backlash from "nimbys"', *The Independent* (30 December 2013).
129 'Nick Clegg to Promise up to Three New Garden Cities with 15,000 Homes Each', *The Guardian* (14 April 2014): http://www.theguardian.com/society/2014/apr/14/nick-clegg-garden-cities-homes [accessed 21 April 2014].

administration's aspirations. Everyone likes gardens so there is a danger that the term 'garden cities' is used as a favourable, cuddly expression and a sweetener to reduce opposition to large conventional developments with little in keeping with Howard's origin vision.[130] As we have seen, to be truly congruent with the philosophy and practical application of Howard's notion of a garden city, a development would encompass the following characteristics:

Robust housing design, combining ergonomic and aesthetic features;
Low density, with ample gardens and accessible green spaces held in common;
Tenures based on community leasing as a safeguard against speculation, or at least embrace affordable pricing;
Provision of self-contained opportunities for work, services and community facilities which are integrated within easy reach of residential zones, rather than a reliance upon commuter-based employment;
In the 21st Century it would also be reasonable to ensure that carbon-zero features and other sustainability-features are also factored into the architectural design, such as the use of passivhaus technology.[131]

None of these characteristics is apparent from the early announcements about a new generation of garden cities, at Ebbsfleet in Kent and at other yet to be specified locations. For example, it has already been conceded that there would be no obligation upon developers to include any allocation of affordable housing, and that a chief attraction of Ebbsfleet is the availability of motorways and rail links into London. We are then left to hope that the greater quantity of houses will itself 'trickle down' to the wider benefit, an unconvincing restatement of the conventional

130 At the time of writing in 2014, a typical example of the vogue for the 'garden' prefix in the West Country is the designation of 'Rowden Park Garden Village' for a proposal for 1, 000 conventional housing units on agricultural land to the south of Chippenham.
131 In this respect developments such as Tomorrow's Garden City, Letchworth (constructed around 2012), with its use of timber frames and hempcrete, are of interest. See Tom Woolley, *Low Impact Building: Housing using Renewable Materials* (Chichester: Wiley-Blackwell, 2013), 68-75.

Conservative argument that economic benefits for the better off will 'trickle down' to all.[132]

So, despite these fresh developments, my initial misgivings about the character of the kinds of new eco-cities or garden cities or suburbs now proposed remain. Their largely technocratic approach may fall short of the broader social vision that Howard projected. The non-separation of workplace and home to forge living, working, integrated environments would also be crucial in any new proposals. The Garden-City Movement favoured the decentralization of self-sufficient communities with amenities and opportunities for creative work nearby rather than the marginalisation of populations in alienated zones between city and country. Howard's ideas embraced a creative synthesis, as he holistically concerned himself with aesthetic and functional aspects of housing design and planning. He gave considerable thought to the social and economic context and the mental and physical health of their occupiers as well as the neighbourhoods and communities in which they lived and broader ecological considerations. His proposal for community leasing, offered a late-Victorian version of a 'third way' beyond municipal or private control, as a self-governing exercise in direct democracy. This owed much to the ideas of thinkers such as Peter Kropotkin and looked forward, via Lewis Mumford and others, to a tradition kept alive in social ecologist ideas about creating a more urbane urbanism, through radically devolved democracy in human-scale communities theorised in such works as Murray Bookchin's From Urbanism to Cities. Kropotkin, in particular, alongside Edward Bellamy, Herbert Spencer and Edward Carpenter, was to influence garden-city ideas, as he urged a more holistic approach to economics, calling for the 'decentralisation of industries' and regretted that 'under the pretext of division of labour, we have sharply separated the brain worker from the manual worker', an approach that had later echoes in E. F. Schumacher's ideas.[133]

132 Internationally, an even more controversial example of the government's 'trickle-down' approach has been the inclusion in the foreign aid programme funding for such mega-developments for the wealthy as the 'Garden City Village' in Nairobi, Kenya. See Claire Provost, 'Hotels, shopping malls, luxury property, Is this the best use of UK aid funding?', *The Guardian* (3 May 2014), 5.
133 Peter Kropotkin, *Fields, Factories and Workshops Tomorrow*, ed., introduced and with additional material by Colin Ward (first pub. as book in 1899 from articles written 1888-90; London: Freedom Press, 1985), 23 and 169.

This pamphlet is largely sympathetic to the aspirations of the garden-city idealists in creating benign environmental conditions and strong design and believes that the model still has potential benefits for more sustainable living in the future. In the present day, however, the opportunities for coordinated community-based, rather than top-down developments are few. I am also cognisant of Jane Jacobs's misgivings about the garden-city's movement and her shrewd observations about the shortcomings of areas that are planned rather than evolve according to the desires of the community itself.[134] It is frequently true that successful neighbourhoods, those that are diverse and intensive, evolve and regenerate from within. In this respect older parts of cities, lived in and endlessly adapted by people's needs and desires, are the most resilient and accommodating; qualities reflected in the fact that older houses and buildings often command the highest prices.

In this respect, reclaiming urban land not used for the commonweal and retrofitting existing housing stock for sustainability will be as necessary for sustainability in the coming decades as sprouting entirely new garden suburbs and eco-villages. A grassroots present-day initiative to make communities more ecologically viable, neighbourly and socially just, is that of Transition Towns network.[135] Again Bristol has been a pioneer as one of the first cities to participate in the process of identifying practical community-based strategies for making localities sustainable and integrated for the coming decades challenged by climate change and constraints upon the use of fossil fuels. As more localised economies re-emerge and the mass commute to work by private car becomes outmoded, Howard's *To-Morrow* may appear less anachronistic. Howard's legacy and impact remains controversial. When considering what might constitute socially viable and ecologically sustainable developments today, however, it would be wise to look again at its most prominent historical prototypes in the theory of Ebenezer Howard and its practical implementation by Raymond Unwin, Thomas Adams and others in the Garden-City Movement.

134 In her classic 1960's study *The Death and Life of Great American Cities: The Failure of Town Planning* [1961] (London: Penguin, 1965).
135 See Rob Hopkins, *The Transition Handbook: From Oil Dependency to Local Resilience* (Bideford: Green Books, 2008) and the website at: http://www.transitionnetwork.org/ [accessed 3 May 2014].

Stephen E. Hunt

Stephen E. Hunt is a writer, librarian, activist and radical historian. He is a co-author of the Bristol Radical History Group's *Strikers, Hobblers, Conchies & Reds: A Radical History of Bristol, 1880-1939* (Breviary Stuff Publications 2014) and also 'Anarchism in Bristol and the West Country to 1950', No. 14 in the Radical Pamphleteer series. He has written for many publications including *Capitalism Nature Socialism, Green Letters, Freedom* and *Environment and History.* Tangent Books published Stephen's latest book *The Revolutionary Urbanism of Street Farm: Eco-Anarchism, Architecture and Alternative Technology in the 1970s* in 2014.